The Elusive Revolution

Anatomy of a Student Revolt

The
Elusive Revolution

Anatomy of a Student Revolt

RAYMOND ARON

Translated by GORDON CLOUGH

PRAEGER PUBLISHERS
New York · Washington · London

Praeger Publishers
111 Fourth Avenue, New York, N.Y. 10003, U.S.A.
5 Cromwell Place, London SW7, England

Published in the United States of America in 1969
by Praeger Publishers, Inc.

© *English translation 1969 by Praeger Publishers, Inc.*
Originally published by Librairie Arthéme Fayard, Paris 1968
as La Révolution Introuvable

LIBRARY OF CONGRESS CATALOG CARD NUMBER: 72-90262

Printed in the United States of America

All that is sham; a revolution made up of memories.
The French Nation is a nation of actors.

P. J. PROUDHON

Notebooks, February 1848

CONTENTS

PREFACE TO THE
ENGLISH LANGUAGE EDITION

Since this book was written—or rather spoken—during the first week of July 1968, the literature of the 'events of May' (the word 'revolution' has disappeared from our vocabulary) has continued to grow. Material of every kind has poured out—historical accounts, pamphlets, sociological analyses, card reading tricks and behind the scenes revelations. The French people are still astounded by their behaviour during those extraordinary days. They are insatiably curious about what happened, although they are more and more inclined—at least until something else happens—to believe that the revolution was no revolution, and that in a sense the event turned out to have been a non-event. 'It is a tale told by an idiot, full of sound and fury, signifying nothing.'

Today we know some essential points and vital dates which make it possible to replace guesses with statements of fact. But this is not enough for us to be able to say 'what would have happened if . . . '

1. Several times in this book I ponder the decision taken by M. Georges Pompidou on his return from Asia, i.e. the unconditional surrender of the government (the re-opening of the Sorbonne, the release of the students, and the promise of an amnesty for convicted demonstrators). Today we know from M. Tournoux's[1] account that the Ministers concerned, M. Joxe,[2] M. Peyrefitte[3] and M. Fouchet,[4] were negotiating with the teachers' and students' representatives before the Prime Minister got back, and that they had hopes of obtaining undertakings from the other side of the table which would balance the

government's concessions. General de Gaulle was very reluctant to make these concessions, but M. Pompidou was able to bring him round to the other point of view—a government which never retreats withdrew completely from the battlefield.

There are still two contradictory interpretations of all this. Was the Prime Minister responsible for allowing the troubles to spread, or did he avert worse things? Some would have it that the fall of the Sorbonne was seen by the masses as a symbol of the collapse of authority. Since the students had won a victory by force over the government, why should the workers hesitate to use the same methods to press their demands? According to this interpretation, the capitulation of 11th May involved such a loss of face for the country's leaders and so discomfited the police, that the spread of the disturbances from the University to industry became inevitable and irresistible.

M. Pompidou himself claims that the decision taken on 11th May prevented the situation from getting even more dangerous. If the Sorbonne had not been open, the crowds who turned out to march on 13th May, the day of the general strike, would have tried to take it by force. Either this assault would have succeeded, or the police would have had had to use their weapons; either event would have been appalling.

I have myself vacillated between these two interpretations. In an article which I wrote on 12th May, and which was published on the 15th, I approved of M. Pompidou's 'surrender'. Subsequently, early in July, I reproached myself for this 'error of judgment'. Today, I can no longer make up my mind. M. Pompidou says that the climate of public opinion made any other policy untenable. It is clear that when he returned, he resigned himself to a long drawn out crisis and the gradual disintegration of the movement to a worm-eaten anarchy, while retaining the hope (which was ultimately justified) that the Communist Party would not engage in insurrection or adventures, and that public opinion would eventually swing back and restore the government's capacity for action. If we accept that this policy was deliberately adopted by M. Pompidou, it was eventually crowned with success, but not without causing severe

x

damage to the prestige of the Head of State. Oddly enough the Prime Minister came out of it with his prestige enhanced. M. Pompidou's insistence in advising the President of the Republic not to cancel his visit to Romania assumes a new significance within the context of this strategy; the contrary advice offered by M. Fouchet, the Minister of the Interior, can likewise be explained by the objections to Pompidou's strategy raised by the three ministers (Joxe, Peyrefitte and Fouchet) who were in charge on the night of the barricades, a strategy which seems to have originated in and was symbolized by the capitulation of the evening of 11th May.

2. At the beginning of July 1968 there was a doubt in my mind concerning the attitudes of the Communist Party from 27th May to 30th May. Were the Grenelle agreements[5] rejected by the rank and file workers or by the Communist Party? We now know with certainty: from 27th May to 30th May, the majority of the Politbureau launched the slogan of a 'popular government'. This slogan implied the overthrow of the Gaullist régime, which the leaders of the Communist Party thought could be achieved *without recourse to insurrection*, for—and on this point M. Pompidou was right—the Communist Party did not intend to set the masses off in an assault against public buildings, on the Hotel Matignon[6] or the Elysée Palace. On Wednesday 29th May, the aim of the mass demonstration was to increase the government's anxiety and to convince it that it was powerless to contain the forces which had been unleashed. For those who confuse *insurrection* and *révolution*, the Communist Party effectively turned down revolution; but insurrection against a French nation which was three-quarters anti-communist, and with the army probably loyal to the legal government, would have involved risks of civil war and chaos which the Communist Party leaders were not prepared to take. Instead, from 27th May to 30th May they were making ready for a 'popular government'; the leaders of the C.F.D.T.[7] who proposed such a government with M. Mendès-France as President, did so not as an overbid from the left, as some people thought at the time, but as a counter to the communist move.

3. The doubts concerning General de Gaulle's intentions when he left Paris on 29th May have now finally been cleared up. He left resolved to organise resistance, but for a few hours Pompidou thought, and feared, that this departure might be final. General de Gaulle, who was less convinced than Pompidou that the Communist Party would behave itself, wanted to be sure that he had enough strength at his disposal to be certain of victory even in the most tragic circumstances. The situation was enough to dissuade the communist sponsors of a 'popular government'. The Communist Party immediately abandoned its slogans of the past few days, and resumed its previous line, that the crisis should be settled economically. It certainly came to regret having departed from this line even for a few days, probably against the judgment of communist trade union leaders.

4. The leftist 'groupuscules'[8] whom I baptised Castroites, Maoists or Trotskyites without drawing any precise distinction between them have now been identified. The ones who played the leading role, after the anarchistic 22nd March movement represented or symbolised by Cohn-Bendit, called themselves Trotskyite. They were the J.C.R. (*Jeunesse communiste révolutionnaire*)—the Communist Revolutionary Youth, and the F.E.R. (*Fédération des Etudiants révolutionnaires*)—the Federation of Revolutionary Students. These two sects, which, particularly at the beginning were divided by personal feuds, acted in common during the crisis, and their militants infiltrated other organizations (U.N.E.F.,[9] P.S.U.[10]). The Union of Communist Marxist-Leninist Students (*Union des étudiants communistes marxistes-leninistes—U.E.C.M.L.*), which was Maoist inclined, neither started the movement nor led it, but merely followed. The Trotskyites claim to be Marxist-Leninist, and dream of reviving the adventure of 1917—the establishment of Soviets everywhere—and they do so in the firm belief that this time it would not end in Stalinism and bureaucratic government.

These clarifications of the attitude of the Communist Party illustrate both the reality of the agreement between the two enemies, the Communist Party and the legal government, and the limits of that agreement; the peaceful co-existence of these two parties is the basis of France's internal order. In all other respects, the interpretation of the 'events' set out briefly in this book still seems to me to be valid. Had I written it, however, a year after the events, rather than a few days after, when I was still in the grip of indignation, I would probably not have expressed myself in the same terms.

The English or American reader should bear in mind that the French University differs in many ways from British or American universities. One essential difference is illustrated by the use of the singular in the former case, and the plural in the latter. Prior to May 1968, the French University was very closely dependant on the Ministry of National Education, the only real management body. No new chair could be created, no funds could be transferred, without the approval of the Ministry. Alongside this administrative centralisation, titular professors had an almost sovereign independence. Neither the Rector of the University, appointed by the Minister, nor the dean of the faculty, nor the heads of department, had any real authority over the teachers. Teaching was subject to the limitations of the national competitive examinations for which all universities had to prepare students, and this imposed on them a degree of uniformity which was hardly conducive to pedagogic or intellectual innovation.

Two other peculiarities should be mentioned. The individual faculties (of sciences, letters and the social sciences, medicine, pharmacy, law and economics) had more reality than the universities themselves. The title Professor of a Faculty, not of the University, is an exact expression of an absurd situation: a professor in one faculty had some difficulty, until recent years, in teaching in another faculty (sociology belonged to the faculty of letters, political economy to the faculties of law and economics). One faculty would put one of its professors at the disposal of another faculty. Sociology students had to cross the rue Saint Jacques to obtain one of the certificates (in political economy) which made up their *licence*. In Paris the faculties had attained such monstrous proportions that the university itself had lost all reality and all appearance of unity.

The *grandes écoles*[11] were outside the University, and attracted the majority of the best of the science and social science students. Other higher educational institutions (the Collège de France, the Musée de l'Homme, the School of Oriental Languages, the Institut d'Etudes Politiques, etc.) were also outside the University proper. The faculties of science, and particularly of letters, tended inevitably to get large numbers of mediocre students, who had passed the *baccalauréat*,[12] who did not know what they wanted to do, but whom the faculties had to accept with no limitations as to their numbers, and irrespective of the resources available to teach them—buildings, libraries or teaching staff.

For many years I have been one of the severest critics of this system. The way in which a career could be decided once and for all by examinations or national competitions passed before the age of 30, or more frequently before 25, in my view led to the formation of a rigid hierarchy which was in many ways deplorable. The way in which higher education was geared to examinations and competitions organized by the Ministry of National Education on a nation-wide basis seemed to me to slow down or to paralyse altogether the essential renewal of methods, materials and research. (I should add that these remarks apply particularly to the faculties of letters and social sciences, to a lesser extent to law and economics. The medical faculties had their own special problems of quite a different kind.)

At the same time, as I am not a Gaullist, there was no good reason why it should fall to me to become the most determined and symbolic opponent of 'the May movement'. Why was I shocked when so many Parisian intellectuals were delighted by what happened? Why was I so indignant when a large number of university teachers, including some titular professors, followed, or in some cases went ahead of the students in revolt? Thinking over this question nearly a year later, I believe I can isolate the motives which led me to react as I did and by which I still stand.

Could any Frenchman for whom patriotism still means anything be a witness of the decomposition of French society, of the collapse of the edifice which has been rebuilt with so much toil after the catastrophe of 1940, without feeling a kind of despair? I come from a Jewish family in Lorraine close to the German frontier. In that background and that area, devotion to France has always been of a special, almost sacred importance. The indifference which everyone, young and adult alike, showed for the fate of the country, shocked me to the very core of my being. I saw with sadness the re-emergence of partisan feelings, which are always so strong; anti-Gaullists delighting in the blow (ultimately perhaps a mortal blow), which the régime had received, without being able to see that the blow had struck France as well. How could a country which was plunged into chaos by a student revolt fail to lose at a single blow the prestige which it had so painfully regained? General de Gaulle's arrogance had angered me rather than convinced me; the violence of his divided opponents brought me back onto his side.

The development of the May crisis was reminiscent of some of the revolutionary adventures of the nineteenth century. Paris, despite the fact that most of the voters in the capital are now converted to moderate political views, rehearsed once again the Great Revolution. I use the word 'rehearse' in its theatrical sense; this was a rehearsal held almost two centuries after the play had been staged. The actors re-ran the play, merely acting, whereas the real actors of 1789, even when they imitated the heroes of the ancients, changed the course of history. Once again the French people obsessed by their memories or the myths of their past, mistook riot and disorder in the streets for a Promethean exploit. If the joint efforts of the students and workers had succeeded in forcing the collapse of the Gaullist Republic, what choice would they have been left with, other than the Communist Party or another Republic—which would either be a continuation of the Fifth with M. Pompidou replacing General de Gaulle, or the Sixth, a bastard product of the Fourth and

Fifth, under M. Mendès-France? Such a revolution seems to me to be unworthy of a great country: it would have been a tragedy if it had given the Communist Party its opportunity, or ridiculous if it had merely changed the number of the Republic and installed a new man in the Elysée Palace.

In this respect my reaction is similar to that of the liberals of the nineteenth century. The most famous of them, Alexis de Tocqueville, while hostile to the established régime, sought the continuity of legal government. They would have found a break in this continuity all the less justifiable since Gaullism, despite everything, is based on universal suffrage and does not violate fundamental liberties.

I was no less shocked by the 'university revolution'—for the student revolt although it did not lead to a political revolution, did in effect provoke a revolution in the university. I was shocked even when the students and the teachers were making valid criticisms and when their demands were well founded. I would like briefly to show how the May disturbances were essentially different from even the most violent outbursts in English or American universities, such as Berkeley, Columbia or the London School of Economics.

Wherever they take place, student revolts produce very varied reactions in the teaching body. In every case there are a great many intermediate positions between unqualified sympathy and unqualified antipathy to the students. Some regret the methods while agreeing that the grievances are just, others consider that although the methods may be regrettable, they are inevitable and ultimately effective, others again are pleased to see their students taking an interest in public affairs, even if this means that their studies will suffer, and so on. At one end of the scale some teachers see student revolt as a conscious and organised attempt to destroy the university order as a means towards destroying the social order itself, while at the other pole, teachers applaud the idealism and nobility of the rebels.

Despite its reputation, this book does not claim to judge the merits of these various interpretations. I have not analysed the various groups of students who took part in the movement.

Although student violence seems to me to be a threat to the continued survival of universities throughout the western hemisphere, my hostility is directed much more against the adults than against the young, against teachers rather than taught, against my ex-colleagues rather than against my ex-students. Nowhere else did teachers take part, as a far from negligible number of French teachers did, in the students' revolutionary action. They shared in the setting up of illegal *ad hoc* assemblies and institutions, and openly or tacitly supported the action of a trade union which refused to regard the government as a valid negotiating body. They were civil servants, but they unconcernedly broke the law and claimed to be acting collectively with the aim of overthrowing the Gaullist Government. Not even the most left-wing teachers at Berkeley or Columbia went as far in their contempt for authority, for common sense, or for the law. In my view the faults of the French University are not enough to justify conduct unworthy of those whose job it is to teach.

This judgment will certainly irritate many of my former colleagues. Some of them talk of the revolutionary tradition, others of the effectiveness of insurrection. Will the reforms which the May movement has made possible, or which it has helped to achieve, justify my severity or show me to have been wrong? It is still too soon to say. Whatever the future may hold, I shall have no regrets for having played my part in the moment of crisis in defending and illustrating the principles on which the liberal university is based. Even if the balance sheet finally shows a profit rather than a loss—a result which is, I believe, unfortunately, doubtful—this must inevitably involve resistance to the idea of turning the University into a political entity, such as is desired by the *New Left*, students and teachers alike, who see themselves as the instrument by which this can be accomplished.

There have been youth revolts, and student revolts in particular, right round the world, from Dakar to Tokyo, and from Berkeley to Rome. They cry out for a scientific study, not for expressions of unreserved support or of unadulterated indignation, both of which are equally pointless. This little book does not claim to be such an objective study; as I said in the introduction to the French edition, it is a personal book, which is less concerned with the student troubles as such than with the national crisis of May to June 1968 and with the enthusiasm shown by grown men who thought they were living, or re-living, a revolutionary epic.

No one can offer any sure interpretation of the moral crisis in the West, a moral crisis which follows a quarter of a century of the most continuous and rapid economic progress of our history. The common factors in all these youth revolts can be explained by some universal causes: a reaction to an obsessional pre-occupation with growth, the appearance of a generation which has known neither war nor the immediate post-war period, which is indifferent to what it has already, and which is impatient for new fields to conquer, the upheaval of higher education as a result of vastly increased numbers of students, and so on. But despite these similarities, university and social problems vary so much from country to country that analyses of what happened in individual nations must precede any attempt at the formation of a general thesis.

It may be, as some of my sociologist colleagues believe, that the elusive revolution is the herald of the collapse of spiritual authority, in particular the authority of the Catholic Church, of the social conflicts of the technological society, and of the dawn of a revolutionary phase once the quarrels of the past have been exhausted. Yet it would seem to me to be prudent, while not excluding such hypotheses altogether, to mention some prosaic truths: the Parisian mob deluded themselves into thinking that they could rebuild society through riots in the nineteenth century as well as in the twentieth. Fortunately on this occasion they have not had to pay as high a price for their period of exaltation as they did in 1848 and 1871. Today as in the past, if we judge on party membership and representation in Parliament, there are only two political forces in France: the Communist Party and the Republic. Finally, the New Left has only two possible futures: either its attempts to use violent means to shake the liberal order in the name of a libertarian ideal will militate in favour of left- or right-wing authoritarianism; or it will arouse the established authorities from their slumber and incite them to make reforms in the universities and in society. In the West the New Left works for Brezhnev or for the Greek colonels, unless it is unwillingly and unwittingly working for those whom it hates most, the *liberal establishment* in the United States and the Republic in France, whom it aims to destroy, but whom it is the historical role of the New Left to renew.

Paris, March 1969

Since this preface was written, General de Gaulle has resigned as a result of the negative response he received from the majority of the Frenchmen in the referendum of 27th April, 1969. There is no doubt that the events of May 1968 are directly —if distantly—responsible for his final retirement in June 1969. After announcing on 24th May that he would hold a referendum, and withdrawing it on 30th May, 1968, Charles de Gaulle finally decided to hold it in the spring of 1969 so as to avoid the appearance of failure, and to show himself and the world at large that the almost mystical links between himself and the French people were still intact. Similarly, the break between the President and M. Pompidou, which weighed so heavily on the régime in its last months, had its origins in the events of May. The blow suffered by the General's Gaullism turned out to be fatal. It remains to be seen whether the French will follow their usual pattern of swinging from one extreme to the other, and will return to the frolics and entertainments of the Fourth Republic, after the ten years of classic theatre of the Fifth.

Raymond Aron   June, 1969

The Elusive Revolution

Anatomy of a Student Revolt

Introduction

WHAT IS THE point of producing yet another book, this time based on transcripts of conversations, about events which are still too recent to be interpreted coolly and scientifically, yet which are too remote for a journalist's commentary to discover anything new about them? The answer is in the title of the book. For weeks on end, Parisian opinion, as if in the grip of some ideological debauchery, seemed to be unanimous in its worship of 'admirable youth', and of the revolution which was not a revolution.

When I published my first article on *The University Crisis*[1] on Tuesday, 11th June, the university premises were still occupied by students, or pseudo-students, holding teach-ins on 'structures' or 'reforms'. Two weeks later, M. André Philip[2] said that he thought what I had said in that article was fair but untimely, because since then the Gaullists had won the elections. There are 'colleagues' of mine who had already accused me of having defected to the winning side, or of supporting the *Civic Action Committees*.[3] This is just one more lie to add to all those which the French people were offered in the place of intellectual nourishment during the month of May.

At the beginning of June no one had yet spoken out against what was happening, and hundreds of letters I received from teachers, students and the parents of school children began with the words 'At last . . '. Someone had finally had the courage to break the conspiracy of silence.

For me to have defected to the winning side, there would have had to have been a winning side to defect to. No victory has been won in society, even less in the University. How will the country ever recover its balance after the shake-up of organizations and hierarchies? How will the economy manage to absorb the wage increases and the reductions in the working week? As General de Gaulle's ideas of participation take shape, will they be influenced by M. Capitant's[4] views? If his views do win the day, the Head of State will have yet another historic exploit to his credit. After having given Algeria its independence on the basis of a mandate given him by those who were in favour of 'Algérie française', he would be giving his blessing to the ruin of private enterprise while his support is drawn from the conservative majority of the electorate. He would certainly derive some ironic satisfaction in giving the lie to the expectations of those who support him without loving him, and on whom, on his side, he relies but does not respect.

Let us assume that the economy will recover from the shock it has suffered during the weeks of May and June. This is a reasonable bet, since industry manages to be both flexible and resilient when challenged. In many areas also the working-class vote revealed resentment against revolutionary leaders or the Communist Party, but not against the Government. Neither the C.G.T.[5] nor the revolutionary *groupuscules* will perhaps manage to set off a second round of wage claim strikes, even if the results of the first campaign inevitably caused disillusionment and bitterness.

The University on the other hand is an autonomous body within the nation; within its precincts sounds from outside are muffled. The autonomy which has been demanded and half obtained could well result in the University becoming still more secluded behind closed doors and blocked-up windows. The electoral defeat of the P.S.U. does not entail a victory for the 'conservatives' or the 'traditionalists' in the universities, the

2

more so since the revolution has apparently revealed to so many 'conservatives' that their minds nurtured latent revolutionary passions, and that the way back to the past or to its restoration is closed for them, for the time being at least.

This book, the first part made up of conversations, and the second of my articles published in *Figaro*, is, like *The Algerian Tragedy*,[6] part of the literature of combat. It is a personal book, which does not set out to explain the truth or the meaning of the event, but merely to remove the mystery from it, to bring it out into the open. My aim becomes quite clear to myself if I open another book put out by the same publishing house but in a different series. This book makes me fully aware of the way in which temperaments can be irreconcilably opposed.[7]

Claude Lefort, a man to whom I was for years linked by a friendship which I believe to have been sincere on both sides, has produced a happy description ('happy' in both senses of the word) of the murder of the liberal University by the March 22nd Movement.[8] 'The student agitators did not boycott the University, they did not call for a strike, they did not stick up lists of demands—or, when they were obliged to announce what their demands were, they announced almost immediately that acceptance of these demands would not stop them. They put the institution into a state where it could no longer operate, they got authority into a position where it could no longer exert itself, they flaunted their illegality in the full light of day and relied on the support of the masses to resist repression. All this they did to such effect that the law came to doubt itself. Indeed, they were free from the danger of repression, for student resistance widened, and dissension spread to the teaching staff, and the administration went mad. As the movement expanded, the truth of the old Leninist formula came to be writ larger and larger: A revolution occurs when those on top can do no more, and when those below will stand for no more.'

I do not dispute the accuracy of this analysis, but I am horrified by the satisfaction it contains. It is true indeed that the agitators from Nanterre 'shook the basic truths on which the system rests, and undermined the unthinking support which the majority of students and teachers gave to the things which made up the reality of their daily existence, and thus dislocated the social bloc of the University'. But the University—indeed any university—needs this spontaneous consensus, this support for basic truths, this respect for unforced discipline. To dislocate the social bloc of the University without knowing what kind of new social structure to build, or with the intention of dislocating the whole of society, is nothing but aesthetic nihilism, or, rather, an outburst by barbarians who are unaware of their barbarity.

Why this enthusiasm for a Cohn-Bendit, the symbol of a 'new freedom'? 'Cohn-Bendit struck the right note when, on the night of 10th May, as he left the Rector's office, he was plied with questions by journalists determined to establish his credentials, and told them: "I have no mandate from anyone, I do not speak in the name of a movement; I say what I believe the majority of students think".' According to Claude Lefort, Cohn-Bendit 'created himself in their image, as they had created themselves in his'; the 22nd March movement 'had no leaders, no hierarchy, no discipline. It disputed with the professionals of *contestation*, and broke all the rules of the game which govern the life of oppositions.' The revolution which made Marxists who had long since broken with Stalinism or Sovietism swoon with delight, was aimed at closing the gap between the leaders and the led, between the hierarchy and the masses. The collapse of the University hierarchy seemed to the revolutionaries to herald the collapse of all hierarchies, since in the University, where students and teachers are set apart from each other by both age and knowledge, the nature of the hierarchy is both rational and unavoidable.

Why was it that cultivated, intelligent men were unable to resist what to my mind was sheer madness? Why were they able at a single stroke to forget the lessons offered by all the thinkers they have read and commented on so eruditely, from Aristotle to Lenin by way of Machiavelli and Marx? Different people have different explanations. Edgar Morin has much sympathy for the student Commune, which in me inspires immediate revulsion—

but we are not merely discussing tastes or colours. At a higher level the May revolution rejected, at least so it seemed, two forms of despotism, on the one hand Soviet style despotism, and on the other the techno-bureaucratic rationality of the 'industrial society'. In reality, however, it failed to prove that 'self-management' of industry, or of the University, or of society, or the ending of the separation of the masses from the leaders, offered any radically original third course between more-or-less liberalised socialism and more-or-less socialised capitalism. Those who sing the praises of the May revolution believe that it went beyond Marxism; but in as far as they have any ideas, those ideas derive from pre-Marxism, from utopian socialism. They have forgotten a hundred years of history, and they ignore the limitations of industrial enterprises and the economy.

They should nevertheless be taken seriously. They will not build a new order, but they have in effect made a breach in the wall of the old order through which other irrational, unpredictable forces may flood. The workers did not know what the slogan 'the factory for the workers' would mean (apart from establishing the authority of the Communist Party), and even after five weeks, the speechmakers of the Sorbonne and Censier[9] did not know what Student Power would mean. If the May troubles lead to an increase in unemployment, however, the young workers will become the shock troops in a revolution as incapable as that of May of constructing a libertarian order, but which might end up by leaving no alternatives other than those offered by repentant Stalinists and redundant colonels. In the same way, students without degrees, or with degrees which are worthless, will not contribute to the renovation of the University, but they may be able—unless the sheep themselves retaliate—to paralyse the operation of some faculties, in Paris if not in the provinces.

In other words, the lessons which I or Edgar Morin or Claude Lefort draw from the May events coincide on one point: the fragility of the modern order. They find this fragility pleasing, while I am disturbed by it. They dream of a libertarian order symbolised by the idea of 'self-management'. This seems to me to be incompatible with modern society, although I do not exclude the possibility of a progressive partial liberalisation of the Soviet type of régime any more than I exclude the possibility of the rational and human improvement of organisations in industry and in the University in France and in every other liberal capitalist society. Edgar Morin and Claude Lefort fear a reform which would lead to the integration of a less anachronistic University in the form of industrial society which the young, and not only the young, members of the bourgeoisie have baptised the 'consumer society'. I hope that what they are afraid of will come to pass, because every other alternative seems to me to be worse. In my view they have fallen into the worst form of utopianism or revolutionary mythology. Although they are more attractive and agreeable than the Communists, they are their intellectual inferiors. If they were to re-read the few political philosophers who really count in the history of Western thought—Aristotle, Machiavelli, Hobbes, Spinoza, Hegel, Auguste Comte, Marx—they would realize this for themselves. For the few days the revolutionary carnival lasts, the state of nature is not without charm; but it rapidly becomes less bearable than any other system of whatever kind. And after a few weeks the Student Commune of the Sorbonne provided yet another proof of this.

In so far as this book is testimony about an event offered after the event itself, and a plea against a myth which is very much alive and a madness which has been sanctified, it does not answer the most serious questions. Countless middle-class families have been torn apart. When fathers and sons meet, not only do they not understand each other, they discover that they do not even speak the same language. Is this a classic and commonplace conflict of generations, or a profound crisis in traditional values? The permissive society has taken the mystery and the poetry out of love. The family, reduced to the parents and children, seems to have been weakened rather than strengthened by the cult of the young, by the freedom they are allowed, and by the way their parents treat them as equals. *Contestation* (argument)[10] flourishes within the Church herself: the 'hierarchy' spoke the language of the revolutionaries without being able thereby to appease the revolt of Catholics on the left.

Those intellectuals who condemn the consumer society most vehemently would not forego what that society alone makes possible—decent living conditions for the greatest number, and hundreds of thousands of students at university. They are just as vehement as they ever were against inequality and injustice, although they know that before the industrial age the national product was distributed even more iniquitously than it is today. They protest, and not without reason, against the reluctance of rich countries to contribute to the development of poor countries. Thus the consumer society has become the dragon to be fought by the very people who possess the benefits it confers.

It is true enough that millions of people have jobs which offer no motive for living; neither production nor consumption can give a meaning to existence. Are the students voicing an, as it were, metaphysical protest against a civilisation which for lack of transcendental beliefs seems to be launched on a crazy adventure in search of greater and greater power and knowledge, but which has no ultimate aim, no discipline of wisdom? If the present phase of history can be defined in terms of ballistic missiles, thermo-nuclear weapons, the moon race and the arms race, should we be surprised that part of the student population wavers between the negation of the hippies, an aspiration towards redeeming violence, and escape towards a new utopia?

The only aim of these brief, superficial observations is to avoid a misunderstanding. It may be that the students, coming themselves from the bourgeoisie, are expressing a *malaise* which is common to the whole of western civilisation. Maybe these libertarians who reject all authority are unwittingly preparing the downfall of our freedoms, by which I mean the downfall of the liberal order, of which the University, with all its faults, was the best guarantor.

Today, at the beginning of July 1968, I refuse to question the sphinx. I am not seeking to speak to the young, who for the most part are not yet ready to listen to what I have to say. As I find myself yet again in opposition to the left-wing intelligentsia, I shall try to explain my position, which is less to fight against men than to fight for ideas.

M. Alain Duhamel[11] has kindly agreed to put to me the questions which he felt were important, and I am grateful to him. Of course, he is in no way responsible for any of my judgments.

was difficult also to write clearly and precisely what I thought of the revolution which was taking place, for the simple reason that newspapers like *Le Figaro* were plagued on all sides, harassed by strikes, and sometimes by the printing workers. And on top of all that, it must not be forgotten that those days, which have since been baptised 'the dawn of liberty' were a period when, for the first time since 1945, some papers came out with words blocked out either by the typesetters or by the printers. Liberty in France has a distressing habit of starting with censorship. Since my so-called 'friends' of the left with their customary good faith are ready enough to call me a 'man of Versailles',[2] I would ask them what they think of a liberty whose first act is to restrict certain freedoms which are regarded as fundamental.

So there was no question of writing about the University at that time. To set out my views of the national crisis, I used what seemed to me to be the most fitting method, which was both the simplest and the most eloquent. This consisted of stringing together quotations from Tocqueville writing on the events of February 1848. These quotations gave the reader an entirely clear picture of my judgment of the chaos which was already being called a revolution. For a time I was undecided whether to use quotations from Tocqueville's *Souvenirs*[3] or *L'Education Sentimentale*. If you know *L'Education Sentimentale*, you will be aware that it has a number of meaty pages on the 'intelligence club'.[4] One can find pages of Flaubert which would probably annoy Jean-Paul Sartre, but which describe far better than I ever could some of the mass movements which arouse such admiration among aesthetes and precious left-wingers.

When we had a government again, after 30th May, I thought that my first duty was to take up a clear position on the university crisis in particular, for reasons that still seem to me unanswerable. As a result of the way my career developed, I am an academic with access to a public forum. Generally speaking I have not written for *Le Figaro* as an academic; although I did occasionally write articles on university problems, I was anxious to make a distinction between my teaching and my work as a journalist, and so I very seldom took advantage of the columns of *Le Figaro* to deal with problems which were peculiar to the University. In the present circumstances, however, the university revolution and the political revolution were so intertwined, and the matters at issue seemed to me to be of such importance, that I would have felt a traitor both to my readers and myself if I had not used this opportunity—an opportunity which I am perhaps the only academic to have available—to air opinions which I knew to be shared, if not by a majority of university teachers, at least by a great many of them.

A.D.   Although you, as an academic and a journalist, managed to get your views heard, apparently the group of academics who shared your opinions managed to keep pretty quiet about them throughout the crisis.

R.A.   Don't be unfair. Those academics who share my views have tried very often in committees and meetings to defend their ideas or their institutions to the best of their ability. But an academic is in a sense disarmed when he comes up against a mass movement. A university teacher by virtue of his qualities and of his faults does not know how to resist the techniques of political manipulation such as were used, either spontaneously or consciously, in a great many faculties. If you like, we can consider in detail the problem of the attitude of academics, of lecturers, of assistants and of assistant lecturers[5] to the various problems of the university later on. But I called my first article 'In the name of those who stayed silent' for the reason that many were indeed reduced to silence. The papers, or some papers, were more willing to publish pieces from organisations which were forging ahead than from organisations in retreat. Don't forget that neither students nor teachers, for the most part, are organised into unions. The S.N.E.-Sup.,[6] the Union of teachers in higher education, has at best 20 per cent of those teachers: this union had no mandate to do what it did. As far as the U.N.E.F.[7] is concerned, no one knows how many students are behind it in times of peace; M. Sauvageot[8] was only an *ad hoc* vice-president. Throughout the weeks of passion or delirium, the voices of only a limited number of ringleaders or organisations could be heard. If the voices of the others were not heard, it may indeed have been that they were not talking loudly enough, I agree, but it is also because they were not invited to broadcast on the non-government radio stations (Luxembourg, Europe No. 1 etc.), and because newspapers did not offer them space. Many academics, indeed, were silent, but the papers and the radio stations were very noisy indeed.

People have said to me 'why did you, who are normally a detached analyst, an observer with aspirations to lucidity, why did you turn into a combatant, and moreover into a combatant on the side of reaction?'

We will be talking about reaction later. I would merely like to say in answer to this charge, which has been levelled at me even by friends, that they don't know me at all well if they think that I have behaved like a detached observer since 1945. After all, what have been the great intellectual battles since 1945?

The first was the debate between the Communists and the non-Communists. I don't think that I was a detached observer in this. *The Opium of the Intellectuals*,[9] which came out in 1955, created just as much furore as my articles on the university crisis in 1968.

In 1957, when I wrote *The Algerian Tragedy*, in which I advocated Algerian independence, which was the probable, and, under certain conditions, almost desirable outcome of the Algerian war, I came under attack even from a left-wing weekly: you know, I really can't win: no matter what I do, I get attacked by the professional leftists. According to this particular weekly, I was giving expression to capitalist defeatism. Some years later it was recognised that this little book on *The Algerian Tragedy* had pointed out the path which history had taken—which is no proof that I was right—and also the path along which those who are in power today had discovered their way out of the situation, the path which was finally taken over by the weeklies of the left. Here too, I don't feel as if I acted as a detached observer.

One other example: there was another great debate about the six-day war and General de Gaulle's press conference. This press conference aroused deep emotions in me, a Frenchman of Jewish origin. There again I took up a firm position in a way which was neither easy nor without risk.

So I feel that over the last twenty years I have always taken a stand when the debate was of sufficient importance to make silence impossible and mere analysis inadequate. I have done nothing in this last crisis which I have not done in previous crises. I have shown what people have called my tendency to analyse without reaching conclusions when writing on economic policy or questions of secondary importance, or when it was a case of having to choose between M. Pflimlin and M. Edgar Faure.[10] I am a good citizen; in other words I obey the legal Government. I usually criticize it because that is the role in which I have cast myself, but I have no reason to give vent to great passions every day of the week.

As far as the 1958 revolution was concerned, I felt myself torn. On the one hand I was deeply shocked by the conditions in which General de Gaulle was returned to power, but at the same time I realized that General de Gaulle might be able to solve the Algerian problem, which at that time was blocking the future development of France. I wrote a little book called *Algeria and the Republic*[11]—my second book on Algeria—which ended with this sentence: 'The May revolution may be the beginning of the political renovation of France, provided that it devours its children with all possible speed.'

A.D.   Yet this time there was a new accent which struck many people who are close to you, and in particular many who have enormous admiration for your analyses even when they do not wholly share the views you express in them. There was an impression that on this occasion, unlike the great debates you have mentioned, and in which you took up a firm position, that on this occasion you introduced a personal note, as if basically there was in this crisis a number of things to which you reacted in an as it were . . .

R.A.   . . . instinctive way.

You are right, and I will answer you absolutely frankly. Everyone lived through this period on his emotions. As far as I

14

know, no-one was calm and lucid throughout these weeks. Personally I lived through those weeks in America in suffering, and in France in indignation—a degree of indignation greater than any I have ever experienced. This was indignation—I admit it to you, and this is a confession—directed against what I believe was unreason. I know of no other period in the history of France which has given me the same feeling that something irrational was happening. I shall try, with your help, to explain this irrationality, but for the moment it put me beside myself because of the disproportion between the legitimate grievances against the Gaullist régime, which I disliked, between the demands of the universities, which I consider legitimate, and this kind of abrupt disintegration of French society. No-one was directly responsible for this disintegration, but the way in which so many people who until then had been close friends of mine hailed this disintegration with enthusiasm and delight induced in me something approaching physical revulsion which showed itself in violent and probably excessive terms directed against certain individuals.

Take the case of a man with whom I was on excellent terms until May—Jean-Jacques Servan-Schreiber. He had written a most successful book in which he pleaded the cause of modernization and rationalism; during the events of May he was gripped by what we might call a libertarian enthusiasm, and he drove me to question which of the two of us had lost his head. I read the university section of *Le Monde* and I wondered 'Am I still in France or—I won't say Cuba because I have no wish to insult Cuba—or in some weird, unknown country?' Can this country which is gripped by collective madness really be France?' I was not the only one to feel this way. Let me read you a letter I received. I won't say who it is from:

'Dear *Archicube*,[12]

'I am taking the liberty of writing to you. Indeed, I have to tell you of my admiration for you. At a time when the entire intelligentsia of France—writers, journalists, academics, priests —are off their heads, you have set out in your *Figaro* articles some basic truths which many students and many teachers, although they are taking part in the performances, deep in their hearts were waiting for. I was out of Paris by chance, because of a long spell in hospital. When I returned, I went back to the *École* and the Latin Quarter. I was disgusted. Please note that I am not an illiterate—*École Normale Superieure*, an arts degree—please note that I am not a fossil—I am 25—please note finally that I am not a dyed-in-the-wool reactionary. What was going on in the *École* struck me as disgraceful. The place was occupied by a handful of teachers and students. And they talked and talked and talked . . . They talked at enormous length of reform and criticized as the fancy took them. In other words they demolished and slandered. It is heart-breaking to hear sociologists saying that they think fraternization with the workers is possible. Have they ever *seen* a worker? Heart-breaking too to hear historians saying that a revolution is possible—have they *read* their history books—or to see school-teachers driving children out on to the streets—do they know what an adolescent is?

'Minds are heated, and intelligent minds drained of meaning. These gentlemen have long since lost touch with reality. The *École* lives in confusion and in Utopia. All this shows you the stupidity of our people. And what I think of the *École* goes for the Sorbonne and Censier and for most of our humanities faculties. So I am writing to tell you that whatever reforms are introduced into our university, whatever reforms, are bound to be harmful if they are formulated by consultation at this time with the staff and the students.'

Something which has separated me from some people who were very close to me before these events was an emotional reaction. I want to admit this reaction, not justify it. A lot of people on the left, people who are deeply anti-Stalinist, felt that in the events of May they had rediscovered the atmosphere of the Soviets of 1917, of the Paris Commune, or even deeper in the past, the Jacobin Commune. And they greeted this discovery with enthusiasm, joy and youthful freshness. They admired the graffiti in the Sorbonne, and they found the young there 'generous, enthusiastic, wonderful'. Everyone has his own emotional reactions,

16

and mine were diametrically opposed. In cases like this, inevitably, everyone creates his own model, everyone mimics his own master and becomes an actor. Right from the start of these events, I argued like this: although these French revolutionaries, that is the P.S.U.[13] and the *groupuscules*,[14] Trotskyite, Maoist and so on, were capable of destroying the existing order, they were incapable of rebuilding a new one. A society as modernized as French society is, cannot, after all, be governed by the libertarian methods of these people, who did not, in any case have any large-scale support behind them. As a result, these revolutionaries drove France to choose between the restoration of order by the Communist Party, or the restoration of order by a strengthened Gaullist or right-wing Government. The compromise solution would have been a Mendès-France Government under Communist control, but this kind of solution could only have been an intermediate stage: such a government under Communist control would have led, as the liberation governments did, either to the elimination of the Communists from government after a period, or to the Communist Party gaining complete power. So the Student Commune, a delight to some people, was profoundly disturbing to me. As a political analyst I could see nothing but misery on the horizon. I found myself in the rôle of Tocqueville on 25th February 1848, accusing his friend Ampère of blindness: 'you understand nothing: you think this movement of the people of Paris magnificent' (or in modern terms: you think this movement of the students magnificent) 'but I tell you that the only possible result of this movement is misfortune', in other words only a strengthened right-wing régime or a popular front type of government dominated by Communism.

That is the way my thoughts ran from the first day of the crisis to the last, and the events ended, as logic said they would, in Gaullism both strengthened by the majority that it won in the subsequent elections and weakened by the resistance from part of the country.

A.D.   There was an article which appeared just before these events which I personally found very interesting and very

17

striking. It was by Pierre Viansson-Ponté[15] and called 'France is getting bored'. I don't think that it was contradicted by what followed at all—in fact, quite the contrary. But don't you have the impression that where in your view there is a decomposition of French society—at least a temporary and superficial decomposition—in which those whose position is crumbling are not the only ones responsible, others see the possibility of a renewal which as always will go through some initial struggles but which might also result in the end in a certain number of reforms which, to my knowledge, you would also like to see.

R.A.   As far as possible I have never excluded the possibility of hope; it is not possible to live through periods like this without from time to time giving oneself up to the illusion or the dream that the worst is not always inevitable. Good can come from evil, after all. In the past France has been willing to carry out reforms when she has had revolutions. Let me quote one incident I am fond of: General de Gaulle was in the chair at a lecture I gave about fifteen years ago, when I said 'from time to time France carries out a revolution, but never carries out reforms.' When I had finished and General de Gaulle was commenting on my lecture, he corrected me very neatly. He said: 'France never carries out reforms except in the course of a revolution'. So when we get on to talking about the long term prospects, I will give partial satisfaction at least to those who accuse me of having a negative attitude. Of course useful, necessary reforms may result from the present crisis, but we were trying to explain my attitude and my indignation.

Going back to this article by Viansson-Ponté. I think that he himself wrote that article without knowing that after the event it would seem to have been a premonition. I will quote my master once again. In January 1848 Tocqueville had made a speech in which he had spoken very eloquently about the tremors which were disturbing French society. He wrote in his 'Souvenirs' 'Now that I am face to face with myself, and I go through my memories to satisfy my curiosity to see if I was in fact as alarmed as I gave the impression of being, I find that I was not. The event justified me more promptly and more completely than I had foreseen. No, I did not expect a revolution such as we were to see—and who *could* have expected it?' Viansson-Ponté would readily agree that when he was writing this article which is now quoted as prophetic, he was unaware of the meaning which posterity would attribute to it. But then perhaps the best prophecies are unconscious. So I thank heaven for the existence of a text which shows us that France was getting bored. Since you like this kind of phrase, there was another one which to me seemed very typical of the French mood and of what sombre spirits like Tocqueville or Renan would have called French frivolity: the slogan on some of the demonstrators' banners; 'Ten years is enough!'

Doesn't this slogan, as a criticizm of General de Gaulle and the Gaullist régime, deserve a place of honour alongside 'France is getting bored'? It seems to me to be one possible explanation or interpretation or expression of the mood of the French people.

A.D.   If we could come back to the basic problem, some people have the feeling that while André Malraux in a sense magnified it by talking of the end of the world, you tended to reduce it, diminish it, by using an expression which I think you have often been criticized for using—*psychodrama*.

R.A.   I did indeed use it in a broadcast on Radio Luxembourg on Saturday, 1st June, when the strikes were still on, two days after General de Gaulle's speech. I also used the expression 'l'immense défoulement'—the colossal release of suppressed feeling. Let's begin with that expression.

What I found one of the most striking phenomena was the teach-in. Parisian, French students talked and talked and talked for almost five weeks. These conversations will glow in their memories. For one thing, everyone praises this aspect of the revolution; 'they've learnt something, they've acquired a kind of maturity through the revolt.' Maybe. How can a veteran dare to judge? I respect my students too much to be convinced that their moral foundation was as deficient as that. A girl from the School of Political Sciences (École des Sciences Politiques) told me that she had discovered that workers existed. So be it. So

19

they talked, and they enjoyed it enormously, which to me suggests something which is confirmed by every sociological study. French students, and especially those in Paris, make up a crowd of solitaries. Many of them genuinely suffer from loneliness, from lack of community life. It's not only a lack of contact with professors who are too remote—which is often true—but also a lack of contact with their fellow students. Some surveys have shown that some students from the provinces have spent years at the Sorbonne without really belonging to any group, without having a circle of friends. This kind of juvenile brotherhood in a semi-delinquent community is over-compensation for the loneliness in which French students normally live. Similarly, most of the reform plans are simply the opposite or the negation of the current French reality. The French labour under a system which is too rigid and a hierarchy which is too authoritarian. Why do they have such an ecstatic recollection of these periods in which they swept everything to the ground? In these crisis periods, when the system is in a state of collapse, they have an illusion of fraternity—and they really feel it—and of equality—which they really experience—and then they reconstruct the hierarchical strait-jacket which encloses them. Ever since 1789 the French have always magnified their revolutions in retrospect into huge parties during which they live out everything they have been deprived of in normal times, and they feel as if they are fulfilling their hopes and ambitions even though it is only in a waking dream. Revolutions like this necessarily look destructive, and are accompanied by wildly extravagant projects and a utopian negation of reality. For instance, the idea of the students becoming their own examiners: no-one really seriously believed in it, but the project aimed to eliminate a system which has a traumatic effect on them, in which examinations are set by some anonymous person whose judgments are categorical and inscrutable.

If tomorrow it was proposed to change the examination system along the lines which I have been advocating for the last fifteen years, I would be in favour of it, as I was yesterday, but at a time when everyone is out of their minds, there has to be someone with the courage to point out unpopular facts. The student community, the vast crowds, those open-ended teach-ins, were all typical of French society: a temporary, evanescent enjoyment of what their society generally denies the French. Certainly, there must be deep underlying causes to produce this kind of phenomenon; but these deep causes are subjective and emotional. It is far more necessary to understand what the actors *feel* rather than to take seriously what they *say*. In fact the methods of interpretation which can be best applied to the present crisis are those which are usually regarded as the most primitive! *Crowd Psychology (La Psychologie des Foules)* by G. Lebon,[16] or Pareto's interpretation by residues.[17] At a time of collective madness, we must try to determine the causes rather than discuss the pseudo-intellectual content of the delirium. No-one can understand what was written in May and June by a number of writers whose intelligence I respect, unless he takes into account the fact that the men of the left, who ever since Stalinism have been cut off from their hopes of Utopia, thought they had discovered something they had always dreamt of, a libertarian revolution, a revolution which would not turn into tyranny and bureaucracy. They relived the days of 1917 or the Commune, and they were deeply hurt by my scepticism or my cynicism. But how can you construct a society on the basis of pre-Marxist socialism or of a mixture of anarcho-syndicalism or Proudhonism?[18] I have nothing against the aesthetes coming to marvel at the Sorbonne and taking part in the students' debate —particularly aesthetes from Avenue Foch,[19] but a carnival has nothing to do with the construction of a new society, a new order, even one confined to the University.

Psychodrama. Of course this expression needs some qualification. But nevertheless everyone of us indulged in rôle-playing during this period. Take me for a start. I have told you that I played the part of Tocqueville, which is not without a touch of the ridiculous, but others played Saint-Just, Robespierre or Lenin, which all things considered was even more ridiculous. Why? The political situation was dominated by a restricted and unwritten alliance between the Communist Party and the

Government. As everyone knows, the Communist Party did not want the large-scale strikes, and even less did it want the general strike to take on a political aspect.

Actually the phrase I just used—alliance between the Government and the Communist Party—is too strong. This is a complex game which has been recognized as such by every observer. It has been easy to see it over the past few years. French foreign policy under General de Gaulle is nearer to what the Moscow leaders want than anything save, perhaps, that of a Communist government. And another thing. In the present world situation, the Soviet Union has too many problems in dealing with so-called socialist régimes on the other side of what we used to call the Iron Curtain, too many difficulties with Chinese-inspired Marxist-Leninist movements in Asia, for it not to fear some unpredictable crisis which might result from the return to power in a country within the American sphere of influence of a Communist Party which would neither blindly follow Moscow's directives nor completely cut itself off from Moscow. The Kremlin leaders were well suited by a France which remained part of the West but whose foreign policy had certain advantages for the Soviet bloc. Don't misunderstand me. In no way do I wish to imply that this foreign policy is against French interests or even the interests of the West. It may be that General de Gaulle's diplomacy simultaneously served the interests of both parts of Europe and of the world. I am merely saying that for the time being the Communist Party prefers General de Gaulle's foreign policy to that which would be followed by a Centre Government or a moderate left Government.

A.D.   You have just changed the subject. You explained why General de Gaulle's foreign policy is far from incompatible with the interests of the Soviet Union, and then you suddenly jumped from the Soviet Union to the French Communist Party. Do you think you can jump so far so fast?

R.A.   That is only half my analysis. The French Communist Party is not now as subservient to Moscow as it was in the previous phase, and several years ago the Party, in view of the world situation and of its own analysis of the situation in

France chose a long term or medium term tactical line. This was first of all to rebuild the unity of the left, which had been broken during the Cold War, and to do so by using the uni-nominal ballot—voting for one candidate only—with two rounds of voting, as unity, once recovered, might be lost again by a return to a proportional ballot. Then they planned to use this unity of the left to escape from the ghetto and to win the recognition of the nation at large as a French Party able to play a part in the political life of the country. These tactics or strategy in the short term excluded the possibility of any revolutionary attempt which the Party leadership considered adventurist. What would happen if there were an attempt to seize power by force? Would the French army stand idly by? Would the anti-Communist majority of the French people submit to the authority of the Communist Party? It has not even been shown that a semi-legal Government under M. Mendès-France or M. Mitterrand would be able to govern without slipping rapidly either towards complete Communist power or towards reaction. A semi-insurrectional Mitterrand or Mendès-France Government would mean the destruction of the strategy chosen by the French Communist Party as a means of entry into national life and of ensuring the election of a left-wing candidate to follow De Gaulle as President of the Republic—something which was far from being wholly impossible in early 1968. After all, M. Mitterrand won 45 per cent of the votes against General de Gaulle in 1965. If this process were to go on peacefully, a Mitterrand type candidate could in due course get himself elected against M. Pompidou in the second ballot. So the Communist Party at the start had no intention of triggering off a revolution, and those whom I have described as the trouble-makers of the P.S.U. could only destroy but could not construct a political base. I would add—and we shall talk about this later—that I was deeply shocked by the P.S.U. because it was largely responsible for bringing Lycée pupils into the political arena. It was the P.S.U. which organized the Lycée Action Committees[20] and brought boys of 14 or 15 out into the streets.

As the Communist Party therefore retained control of the mass of the workers and had no intention of mounting an insurrection, it really is a psychodrama with which we are concerned. M. Sauvageot or M. Geismar[21] talked and acted like leaders of the Paris Commune of 1789 or 1790, or like the *ad hoc* leaders of February 1848, but in quite a different context. Getting rid of a president elected by a universal vote is a very different matter from getting rid of a king. Moreover these *groupuscules* and agitators represented neither the masses of workers nor the French people. The P.S.U. is a party of intellectuals, and the groups of young Leninist-Marxist revolutionaries, Maoists, Castroites and so on, are nothing really but *groupuscules*. Paris once more in its history, almost had a revolution, and then ended as usual by voting Conservative; everyone involved imitated their great ancestors and unearthed revolutionary models enshrined in the collective unconscious. It was a psychodrama rather than a real drama because of the absence of a revolutionary party, right up to the moment in time when the apparent disintegration of power aroused widespread alarm; it was a psychodrama rather than a real drama also because it all happened without physical violence. The most striking thing about it was the verbal delirium, with no one killed.

Nineteenth-century revolutions claimed few victims in their first phases, but there were some deaths. In 1968 the holocaust began after the revolutionary period when petrol came on sale again and motorists got back on the roads. But during those weeks when the revolution was the word, the most passionate revolutionaries respected the life and physical security of their enemies. Is this a psychodrama or a civilized revolution? 'So the lukewarm passions of the time were given voice in the inflamed language of '93, and there were constant references to the example and the names of famous scoundrels, whom no-one had the energy, nor even a genuine wish, to emulate.' (Tocqueville)

Another phenomenon which struck me was the way in which the revolutionary fever abated in a mere half-hour. You remember as well as I those days between the Monday and the Friday, that is after the Billancourt workers had rejected the Grenelle agreements,[22] either spontaneously, or as a result of the action groups and the young workers, or because certain members of the politburo, like M. Barjonnet,[23] judged that they now had an opportunity of going further than they had initially intended. There was a strange atmosphere from Monday to Friday: rats left the sinking ship; some Gaullist deputies begged the Prime Minister to resign or to persuade the President of the Republic to resign. In Paris at least almost everyone was in the grip of a kind of delirium. The French people, and certainly the people of Paris, felt that the State had disappeared, that there was no Government any more, and that once more anything was possible. Yet nothing serious happened.

'We have been through so many years of insurrection and revolt that a kind of special morality has grown up among us, a code of conduct peculiar to periods of civil disturbance. Under these special laws, murder is tolerated, but theft is strictly forbidden, which nevertheless does not prevent a lot of thieving from going on at these times, for a society of insurgents cannot be expected to be different from other societies within which there are always villains who could not care less about the morality of their society, and for whom its honour code goes for nothing when no-one can see them' (Tocqueville). Revolutionary morality has advanced over the last hundred-and-twenty years: today it prohibits murder as well as theft. Nothing remains but a symbol of violence and a challenge flung down to the forces of order, who are denounced if they resort to repression, and discredited if they lose their self-restraint. For three days the French people had a physical sensation of the absence of authority. Then General de Gaulle spoke for three minutes, and within the next half-hour the President of the Communist Group in Parliament said 'we agree to elections.' The whole affair was over, and the atmosphere transformed. A speech was enough to abate what had been called a 'revolutionary' fever. It was from all this that I derived the impression, for which I have used the word 'psychodrama'. The French had played out a kind of vast charade for themselves: in an age when revolutions of the 1848 pattern no longer make sense, they put on the spectacle of a great revolution. Then a man stands up and speaks, and the comedy is over.

A.D.   You have said yourself that General de Gaulle's speech rang down the curtain. It was quite remarkable that this speech reintroduced a policy line and revived the structures of government. So at least two problems are raised. The first is, how was it that there was no plan of Government action *before* the speech? If there had been, then the 'comedy' might have ended earlier. Again, there was the possibility, which General de Gaulle spoke of himself, when he confirmed that on the day before his speech he had not thought only of taking an initiative, but purely and simply of resigning. And if he had done that, the 'comedy' might well have gone on.

R.A.   That's true, but I am not convinced that General de Gaulle really considered resignation. I am not convinced that he himself was not affected by a kind of intoxication, but let us accept that he did think of resigning. I will argue without hesitation that a revolution of this kind is still possible in France because of the fragility of French institutions. It is for that reason that I take these events seriously. I by no means exclude the possibility that in certain circumstances the psychodrama could have turned into a real drama. But I maintain that had the psychodrama ended with the departure of General de Gaulle and the substitution of a Mendès-France Government, we would have seen a process typical of French revolutions, an inevitable process. We would have had a left-wing Government more or less under the control of the Communist Party, inevitably turning after a certain time either into a completely Communist-controlled Government, or, more probably, leading to a violent reaction. Instead of the affair ending quietly, and so far without anyone getting killed and without a political upheaval, we would have gone through the various stages of nineteenth-century revolutions. First we would have had a government of the extreme left, like the provisional government of 1848, then either brutal repression or a gradual slide towards moderation. So, although I am not a Gaullist, although I am still not a

Gaullist, and although I continue to enjoy the peculiar antipathy of the General, I was delighted, as most Frenchmen were,
by his speech on 30th May, for in my view it was preferable at
the time for the crisis to be ended by General de Gaulle rather
than by Mendès-France, which would probably have happened
if General de Gaulle had retired.

So left's come on to the real question: how could this psychodrama have become a real drama? How could this tragi-comedy
have ended as a tragedy?

On this I shall just throw out at random some ideas which
have come to me since May 1968 while thinking about this odd
performance.

In developed industrial societies the fundamental conservative force is the trade union movement. Why are we quite prepared to say that revolutions in the style of the nineteenth century
have become, if not impossible (personally, I have never gone
as far as that) at least less probable in modernized societies than
in societies in the process of modernization? The main reason is
the conservatism of trade unions in the United States, in Scandi-
navia and the Federal German Republic. The trade unions
make demands, but they are not revolutionary. They want to
improve the conditions of the workers, and they demand ultimately a larger say in the control of industry, but they do not
envisage the violent overthrow of a democratically-elected
government because they are aware of the complex systems
needed for the management of a concern. They know that any
disturbance, any violent upheaval, inevitably leads to lower
production, and consequently a decline in the standard of living
of the people they represent. Unlike the gilded youth of the 16th
arrondissement, they are in favour of the consumer society.
Trade union leaders in most modernized countries fight in the
first place for improvements in the conditions of the workers and
ultimately for some participation, either as a pressure group at
government level, or as a group with a degree of partnership in
the running of an individual firm. They are not in favour of
revolutionary movements. Now here we come up against one of
the French eccentricities! In normal times most workers in

France are not union members. As you know, fewer than 20 per cent of French workers are paid-up union members. French trade unionism is a minority unionism, and moreover the most powerful union is linked with the Communist Party. It may be that the union linked with the Communist Party is no longer revolutionary, but it cannot admit that it is not. As a result of the history of the French working class, workers in France are not integrated into modern society in the same way as are the majority of workers in Britain, Germany and the U.S.A. When there is a great wave of demands, the working class rediscovers revolutionary reflexes or emotions: the red flag or the black flag. What proportion of workers respond to such slogans, symbols or activities? I don't know, but the fact is that our trade unions are not a buffer against revolutionary movements, as are the German Social-Democrat unions or the Labour unions in Britain or the U.S.A. This explains why the university revolution was able to make contact with the French working class, whereas up to now there has been scant sympathy between workers and students in the U.S.A., in Britain or in West Germany. Would solidarity between students and young workers emerge elsewhere? I don't expect so. But the fact remains that French society is so vulnerable because of the weakness of intermediary negotiating bodies; and one of the most specific weaknesses is the fact that the majority of workers are not unionized, which leaves the field clear for minorities in times of crisis.

You find a comparable phenomenon in the universities. The professors who are not of the left are on the whole not unionized. Autonomous unions contain numerically rather more university teachers than the S.N.E.-Sup. and mainly include professors, whereas most further degree or graduate teachers have no interest in unions. This general shortage of intermediary bodies has allowed minority unions to play a spectacular part both in the university and in the working class.

Another phenomenon which I noticed was the survival of the tradition of the overthrow of authority by riot. The French nation has not yet rid itself of the revolutionary virus; or, if you prefer, it still retains a revolutionary freshness of spirit. In the

28

absence of a ministerial crisis, the French people accept that street movements can make and un-make governments. There have been so many cases of this since 1789 that even in Government departments the civil servants accept new masters at a day or two's notice. 'I noticed a universal effort to come to terms with the event which fate had fashioned, and to tame the new master' (Tocqueville). On this occasion the old master returned, and so we had a case of the biter bit.

This attitude of the French people was certainly one of the causes of the sometimes dramatic nature of the May events in Paris. In the capital at least there was an awareness that people were ready to accept whatever government emerged from the psychodrama—which in those circumstances would have become a genuine drama.

There is one other cause—the weakening of the Communist Party by the action of revolutionary groups. The Communist Party has always been afraid of being overtaken on the left: it always reacts by trying to regain control of the movement by broadening it. It did not want a general strike, but when the first strikes developed with the occupation of the factories, it triggered off major strikes so as to swamp the activist minorities. The Communist Party, which wanted to avoid a revolutionary situation, contributed to the creation of one in order to retain control of the movement. In order to fend off the breakthrough on the left it was forced to escalate the strikes until—on the Monday or Tuesday after the Grenelle agreements—a part of the politburo of the Communist Party may even have come to the point of expecting the collapse of the régime and the election of a popular front government including the Communists. The Communists could hardly be more Gaullist than de Gaulle, or try to save a power which seemed not to be defending itself: 'we cannot be less revolutionary than the 16th arrondissement: if they absolutely insist on giving us power, we will not refuse to take it.'

A.D.   There are two comments I would like to make. First, especially after the Grenelle agreements, public sympathy with the revolutionary movement cooled off, as the opinion polls showed, and people who initially had cheerfully accepted everything that happened, particularly as long as the crisis was confined to the University, became increasingly worried: so there was a split between the small minorities who were out on the streets and the vast majority who stayed silent. And also—as there always is, and you know that better than I—a very striking split between Paris and the rest of the country.

R.A.   I entirely agree with you. During the first week the parents of the students were hostile to the police. After all, if there is a row, parents automatically back their children against their teachers.

In the next week they went along to the Sorbonne Commune, and they found it an exciting show. They were torn between admiration for their children—the cult of youth is a way in which adults can delude themselves into thinking they are still young—and fear of the social consequences. In the two weeks when the crisis seemed to be essentially a university crisis, conventional public opinion in Paris, was undecided. Then when we came to the quasi-general strike, opinions changed. After the Grenelle agreements had been rejected by the workers, those responsible for running the French economy gauged the scale of the economic catastrophe. And simultaneously another striking phenomenon manifested itself—a kind of disintegration of hierarchies: the university hierarchy dissolved into plenary assemblies of all grades of staff or general assemblies of staff and students; in some firms a bourgeois semi-revolution or staff re-volt, developed. Middle and senior personnel rose against a hierarchy in which they felt they did not participate and which tended to ignore them. In part this was a backward-looking revolution, in part forward looking. In one sense it was a nos-talgia for a pre-modern society, and in another it was an aspira-tion towards more modernity, towards greater communication and more participation. But to come back to the problem we are concerned with; the collapse of university hierarchies was followed by the collapse of many hierarchies, a typically French phenomenon which can only be explained by the weakness of the negotiating links between the top of the hierarchy and those below it, and by the way in which individuals are unused to co-operating among themselves outside the framework of a bureaucratic hierarchy. When the keystone of the whole society collapsed, when the Government seemed to have ceased to exist, society broke up in the same way as the State. Social disintegration, at least an apparent disintegration for some days, was followed after a few weeks by a difficult, incomplete and haphazard rebuilding of the former structure. What was there before had to be rebuilt, even if it meant creating something else later. The University goes on struggling, and continues its revolution in the midst of a society which is in the process of moving out of the revolutionary phase.

Now we come to the incompetence of government.

As regards the Government, that is to say General de Gaulle and his aides, the observer has a choice between condemning them for their tactical errors and being grateful to them for the final victory. So let us try to be as impartial as possible. In the first week, on the first day, no-one took the comings and goings at the Sorbonne and Nanterre[24] very seriously. Everyone agrees that the closure of Nanterre became inevitable because a small group of *enragés*—out-and-out extremists—wanted *to force* the university authorities into taking repressive measures. There was a lot of argument about the police going into the Sorbonne, I shall not hark back to this point. Even if it was not necessary, as most people say, it would have become so a few days later. As soon as a few students wanted to force the authorities to take repressive measures, no-one could stop them. Street demonstrations followed by convictions in summary courts, and convictions of demonstrators pulled in at random by the police and given jail sentences, angered the students and created a factitious solidarity between teachers and students against Authority. Then followed the 'police brutalities' which the doctrinaires of violence had sought, and against which they protested.

From the 3rd to the 11th May M. Pompidou was in Asia. On the night from Friday to Saturday there were negotiations via a radio station, a great deal of hesitation and then the order to destroy the barricades, followed by scenes of violence which some blamed on the demonstrators who had raised the barricades, and others on an excess of zeal by the police. Politically the night from the 10th to the 11th was a catastrophe because it forged a superficial unity between the majority of teachers and the majority of students against the police and the Government. M. Pompidou came back, tried a wager, and lost. He wagered that by capitulating he would bring the disturbances to an end. I do not condemn him for this. At the time I was inclined to think he was right, but in retrospect I am rather ashamed of this view. Historically, he was wrong. Most probably concessions should have been made *before* the night of Friday to Saturday: *after* that night, capitulation led to new agitation and gave birth to the Student Communes. Capitulation, the fall of the university Bastille, the Sorbonne in the hands of the victorious students: these were in effect the symbols of a revolution. The symbol, that is, of a pseudo-revolution because student power and the power of the workers have nothing in common.

Once the Student Commune was established, the Government decided to tolerate it, and most university authorities came to accept or follow the student revolution in some form or another. This was such an astonishing phenomenon that the Government itself did not understand what was going on, and did not know whether it was faced with a psychodrama or a real event. Then there was a day of general strike, and the Government made another mistake by letting General de Gaulle leave on his visit to Rumania. During the first week the Prime Minister tours Asia, and in the second the keystone of the system, the President of the Republic, gets cheered by Rumanian students while French students are barracking him back home. Everyone can still remember the impression all this produced in France. General de Gaulle came back and decided to wait and let things rot. He was face to face with a Student Commune which he could not put down without using force, which at that time was unthinkable: there were major strikes which might have been spontaneous or not, which he did not find seriously disturbing, because he was relying on the Communist Party to avoid a revolution.

32

Then the wavering began: it seems that he let himself be persuaded not to speak at once, but allowed the parliamentary debate to grind on, and a new atmosphere was at once perceptible in the Assembly. Some parliamentarians already scented a change of government, perhaps even a change of régime. Then he made the disastrous referendum speech of 24th May: it seemed as if we were listening to the phantom of a spectre or the spectre of a phantom. He proposed a referendum which the *Conseil d'Etat* immediately and courageously declared to be unconstitutional. Economic activity was at a standstill, but the Communist Party did not promote a strike of electricity workers, which would have seriously aggravated the situation. According to traditional mythology, a general strike was bound to be in the spirit of revolt, but the Communist Party aimed to put an end to the strikes by agreements similar to the Matignon agreements[25] of 1936; so it adopted the techniques used by trade unionists *vis-à-vis* the popular front Government, but used them *vis-à-vis* a Government to which it was declaredly hostile, and which it denounced daily as being a Government based on personal power. M. Pompidou, convinced of the good intentions of the Communist Party, negotiated the Grenelle agreements in a similar hope of settling the strikes by methods comparable with those of the Matignon agreements. Then came Monday, and the rejection of the agreements. At this point everyone wondered whether the Communist Party, carried away by events, had been led to change its tactics, or whether it really remained master of its troops. At this moment everything seemed to be in the balance, and fate hesitated, maybe in reality, maybe only in appearance. One genuine revolution—the university revolution, —and one pseudo-revolution—the social movement—between them came close to provoking a change of government or régime.

The psychodrama called into question the revolutionary propensities of the French people, the weakness of the *corps intermédiaires*, the intermediary negotiating links, accentuated by Gaullism in which everything depended on General de Gaulle in person, the power of irrational forces in a so-called modern

33

society, and probably the dissatisfaction of many Frenchmen during a period of modernization, when deprived of the morphine of inflation. The French therefore had enough frustrations, resentments and grievances to ensure that when circumstances were right a colossal release of suppressed feeling would result.

Was this the end of a civilization?

One lesson which I draw from these events is that modern societies are more fragile than we think. The University, which we shall be talking about later, is a particularly fragile institution. And I repeat that the reason I have spoken and written with some passion is that these young people and many of my colleagues are destroying a precious institution because they are shaking its moral foundation. The University's only moral foundation is the reciprocal tolerance of the teaching staff and the voluntary discipline of students. There can be no more higher education if students use the University as a forum for political agitation. This would be equivalent to the Latino-Americanization of French universities—the ruin of the universities. Whatever part students take in the running of the University, and particularly if it becomes a large part, voluntary discipline of students will become an increasingly indispensable condition of its survival. My colleague Touraine[26] has written that anyone who opposes this revolution abdicates the right to claim that he is in favour of reforms. To this I say mildly but firmly that *this is the exact opposite of the truth.* No worthwhile reforms in the University can be carried out except in the context of the restoration of the University's moral foundation. I am afraid that this restoration may take several years: perhaps new universities will have to be created, and those of yesterday are dead. The fragility of the University as an institution is well known, and that is why I spoke out immediately against the violence, and against both the young and old extremists. These people acted rightly if they were trying to destroy the University and society, but if all they wanted was reform, they were wrong, for what they did was to make the life of a liberal university virtually impossible for quite a long time to come. I would add that the non-liberal university, of the Soviet pattern, is run on much stricter lines.

The fragility of society itself varies from country to country, but any pluralist society, and perhaps even, any modern non-pluralist society, has within itself elements of weakness. Rather like a university, a factory relies on a semi-voluntary discipline from those who work in it. A production line demands that all the workers on it carry out their individual jobs properly. A research department does not think under police protection. A factory, or society, lives and prospers thanks to multiple and complex co-operation between a large number of individuals without there being any possibility of resorting constantly to force, the ultimate sanction of any social order. In this sense I see the University as in a way the microcosm of society as a whole. Social organization will decompose on the day when individuals refuse to accept the solidarity and division of labour, and refuse to submit to the order imposed by all on all.

Why should this be felt more in France than elsewhere? Because France is simultaneously nostalgic for the life of grand-papa, and insufficiently modernized. All the criticisms levelled at France, have an element of truth: aspiration to modernity and rejection of modernity are intermixed. So are the anarchist dream and the dream of the post-industrial society. End of a civilization, says Malraux. What holds together societies which have no basic beliefs? That is an old idea which has been exposed by Spengler, Toynbee and others; all known civilizations have lived within the unity of one religion; they were cemented by collective belief, but now, modern Western civilization has lost the religious consensus. That idea was first set out by August Comte.[27] Since the Nanterre sociologists played such a large part in this crisis, let us recall that the great sociological theories born at the beginning of the nineteenth century drew their inspiration from the theme of religious disintegration of modern societies. Is there a necessary progression from the absence of a common religion to processions of workers, the symbol of the end of the world? I am terrified by these great sweeping bird's eye view perspectives. If this diagnosis of world history is well founded, workers' strikes are only a feeble symptom of it.

In recent years there have been widespread instances of minor outbreaks of violence, riots, a youth revolt, civil disturbance in the cities of the United States. It seems that major wars, ruled out by the means of destruction available to the great powers, have given place to minor wars, and sometimes even to large scale minor wars, as in Vietnam. Within nations, structural and traditional ideologies like Marxism or liberalism are in decline, but this weakening is accompanied by a revival of pre-Marxist ideologies like proudhonism or libertarianism, and also, on the other hand, by a kind of cult of violence. During these last years a philosophy of the absurd has flourished in a new form in literature, in philosophy and in the cinema. This philosophy, instead of ending up in Sartre's pro-Sovietism or Camus' moralism of the fifties, has ended in 'guevarism', the guerilla expression of a virile and revolutionary attitude. Small groups have appeared in every country, in the U.S.A., in Germany, as well as France, calling themselves Students for a Democratic Society. They are much like our French extremists, destroying for destruction's sake, and pride themselves on having no defined objectives and no clear views on the society they want to build. Is this the proof that our societies, having lost their belief in transcendental religions, and having experienced a weakening of their belief in ideologies, are in the process of disintegration? Maybe, but for the moment the most reasonable diagnosis seems to me to be that there is an alternation of periods—those of seeming tranquillity, when individuals enclose themselves in the cares of professional life and family life, and those of agitation. I am attracted by two explanations for this, one quasi-biological or psychological, and the other sociological. The first emphasizes the fact that for the life of society to remain peaceful, requires a kind of repression of aggressive impulses. Even freedom of sexual habits does not lead to the satisfaction of desire. To use the language of Marcuse, society remains oppressive, or that of Konrad Lorenz, man, an aggressive animal, needs to express his aggressiveness.

The sociological explanation stresses the alternation of phases. The individual is apparently reduced to the condition of a private person, not belonging to any community of religious faith or political belief and then these isolated people, so keen on comfort and prosperity, are suddenly gripped with wild passions. They fall victim either to a fever with definite aims which end in political or social upheavals, or a fever with no definite aims, such as in the present case. Unless we have a model which matches our aspirations then outbursts of fever are essentially negative, nihilist or destructive. What model is there which would fit the aspirations of revolutionaries, considering that the Soviet model is super-bureaucratic? The genuine revolutionaries of May swore by direct democracy, which in one sense is more anti-Soviet than anti-capitalist. Yet they claim to believe in Marxism, which is a paradox, inasmuch as it is difficult to see how a planned society can be less bureaucratic than a semi-liberal capitalist society. True enough, the latter includes a bureaucracy in each firm as well as a State bureaucracy, but a planned society gives even less free rein to liberties, to people, and to initiative. We should not forget, when taking all this seriously, the Ubu-esque[28] and the peculiarly 'Parisian' aspects of the May events, Jean-Luc Godard and the cultural revolution at the Cannes film festival, and the progressive writers taking the Hotel Massa[29] by storm. We are back to the psychodrama, back to the caricature of the revolutionary comedy.

37

2

The Revolution
within the Revolution

R.A.   I would like to break the rules of our conversation by suggesting myself the title which I would like to give to our second chapter, or our second discussion. I would like to call it *The Revolution within the Revolution*, which is not my phrase, and which has a meaning very different from the one which I want to give it, but which seems to me to be well suited to the phenomenon we have observed.

A.D.   What then do you mean by 'Revolution within the Revolution'?

R.A.   I would suggest this very simple interpretation. What we call the May revolution—(in the coming months the intellectuals will stage a great debate to establish whether there was a revolution or not, and already the more moderate prefer to call it 'the events of May')—began in a student revolt. The first event which public opinion saw as being revolutionary was the occupation of the Sorbonne by the students on Monday 13th May, the day after M. Pompidou's return and his attempt at appeasement. Throughout May and the first part of June, the University experienced its own revolution, which is still going on now that the threat of social revolution—assuming that such a threat ever existed—has for the moment disappeared. By

38

'university revolution' I mean the attempt made by a certain number of students, with the encouragement and support of some teachers, not merely to discuss desirable reforms, but to establish a new system of administration by means of a real revolt. In the best French tradition a Constitution for the universities of the future was drafted, but even before there was agreement on the form of this Constitution, revolutionary bodies were established, with plenary assemblies taking the place of professorial assemblies. These plenary assemblies include all teachers from assistants to full professors, whereas the old assemblies were made up of professors and delegates of the *assistants*[1] and the *maîtres-assistants*;[1] the general assemblies included students as well as teachers. Students and teachers voted together, and often used block votes to determine the representation of the various groups (in the revolutionary assemblies, students took part in the voting to appoint representatives of the teaching body). The students and some of the teachers used illegal methods to establish a new *de facto* organization in which some of them firmly believed and which they hoped would win the blessing of the Government. This was a private revolution which took place within the University, conducted along lines borrowed from political revolutions.

A.D.   There are several problems connected with the University, about which you have views. Perhaps you could develop some of them now.

R.A.   I would like to say a few words about a subject which all commentators have remarked on—the way in which the revolts of this kind have happened in most parts of the world. The American humorist Art Buchwald wrote the most amusing piece about this: when the Polish students revolt, the American establishment is overjoyed; when American students revolt, the Russian establishment seizes on it with delight to denounce capitalism. We are sympathetic towards student rebellion in eastern Europe, and the Soviets derive a certain satisfaction, and perhaps a little anxiety, from student rebellion in the West.

The similarity of these problems shows that the malaise of

youth in general, and of student youth in particular, must have some common causes. But we must draw a distinction between the revolt of students who seek freedoms already guaranteed in the West, and the kind of student revolt which would end up by suppressing those freedoms, perhaps in spite of the rebels themselves. People who say 'it makes no difference what the grievances, the ideologies or the aims are', are fundamentally nihilists. There is similarly an element of nihilism in the interpretation which claims that the student revolt is merely a rejection of industrial society, whether that society is the Western or the Soviet version. This is not to say that the revolts of these various groups of young people against certain aspects of the industrial society have nothing in common, but if this interpretation is valid—which I believe it to be in part—we are in the presence of a phenomenon which is as much biological as social. I shall stress two main factors.

The situation of students has become increasingly peculiar or separate from all other social groups. If boys and girls who reach physical and human maturity at the age of 14 or 15 have to continue their apprenticeship until they are 23 or more, this involves a kind of contradiction between their self-awareness and their position in life; no matter what is done about it, this is bound to be largely a dependent position, from which the responsibilities of adult life are for the most part excluded. These boys and girls are condemned to learn and to take examinations —occupations which they see as childish. This situation was just tolerable as long as it involved only a small number drawn from the privileged classes. No one gave any prior consideration to the socio-biological consequences which would result from the admission of masses of students, of crowds hundreds of thousands strong of boys and girls who had reached maturity but who were obliged to continue to live as children or semi-children.

The first outburst came at Berkeley, which is comparable in student population to the University of Paris. The monstrous defects of the University of Paris make it a caricature of the French system. 130,000 students, even if some of them are not really studying, all crammed into one large city, is way beyond the tolerable density. As others before me have done, I shall refer to biological studies: we know that when rats or other animals are forced to live at an excessive density in a confined space they begin to show all the signs of mental anguish which in a human being we would see as symptoms of neurosis. Students in France, and particularly those in Paris, suffer from an over-population neurosis produced by too many of them being confined in too small a space. This may not be a very romantic interpretation, but if we want to understand the May revolt we would be wrong to pay too much attention to what the young people said; we must isolate and discuss the emotional states which lay behind their words and their deeds. We will get nowhere by attempting to hold rational discussion with people intoxicated by their own exploits. Let us try to explain the circumstances in which these students, who were all set for adventure, lived through the psychodrama. Their initial burst of enthusiasm was extraordinary, but it gradually turned into growing anxiety; perhaps tomorrow, when they remember the dream, they will experience the bitterness of disillusionment.

Now, since you ask, I would like to come back to the criticisms which were commonly made about the French University as it used to be. These are criticisms which I have made repeatedly over the last fifteen years. Since these ideas are now commonplace and generally accepted, I will go quickly through them.

We did not really have *universities*, we had the *University*. Every faculty, every university, was in effect managed by the Ministry of National Education. No university, no faculty, could create a new chair or draw up its own syllabus without the Ministry's financial approval and support. The result of this was a grotesque uniformity, which in the faculties of letters was curiously enough aggravated by the Fouchet-Aigrain reform,[1] even though the purpose of this had been, quite genuinely, to promote the diversification of faculties. Its intentions were frustrated by the administrative machinery. In fact the Fouchet-Aigrain reform, i.e. the replacement of the traditional certificates by annual programmes, led to every professor being forced to follow the same syllabus and all students to take the same examinations for the first two years, at least in the faculties of letters. There had never been such a severe restriction of autonomy in the preparation of syllabuses.

The faculties of letters, sciences and even of law and economics (the problem in the medical faculties seems to me to be rather different) prepared their students for examinations held at a national level. C.A.P.E.S.[1] and the *agrégation*[1] examination were organized by the Ministry of National Education for every university in France. Therefore the universities were obliged to prepare students who wanted an academic career, and in particular all those who wanted to try for very high qualifications, for identical examinations. There is room for discussion as to the harm or good which these national titles do; but it is a fact that competitive examinations at the national level impose uniformity on the universities. A great many proposals for autonomy will have no sense as long as there are fixed rules for the first four years, i.e. for the *licence*[1] and the *maîtrise*,[1] and for the national competitive examinations.

The education offered by the faculties of letters mainly, but also up to a point in the science faculties, laid a considerable stress on general culture or on pure or theoretical science. In most of the traditional disciplines, the teaching tended to produce teachers. Students who graduated from the faculties of letters with a *licence* in history, sociology or psychology, had no diploma which qualified them for immediate employment in a specific profession. The larger the student population became, the greater was the anguish caused by the lack of career prospects for graduates. The University went on accepting more and more students and persisted in refusing to consider what sort of jobs they would be able to find. The responsibility must be shared by the universities, the ministry, and in part by the students themselves. If students claim to be capable of adult behaviour and want to argue with their teachers (and why not?) they, or their families, should also give some thought to their future. Today there are three or four candidates for every place in the C.A.P.E.S. or in the mathematics or physics *agrégation*. I am told that even in the science faculties many graduates fear that they will not be able to find work outside the University. This is a truly shocking phenomenon in a society which is so short of scientists. If our scientists are worried too, this must be because the education given in the universities is not adapted to the needs of the economy. The revolutionaries object that to temper the education given to the needs of a capitalist régime is to accept a technocratic university, but one really cannot go on refusing to pre-select candidates for admission to a university, rejecting the adaptation of the education offered to the needs of the professions, and then complain later of the lack of outlets. As long as everyone who passes the *baccalauréat* can go automatically on to university, they must understand that an increase in culture is a benefit in itself, and that it does not constitute a guarantee of employment. Here again, I think that we should not take the students' statements too seriously. It is clear that the majority of students, once they have their degree in their pockets, want a chance of doing a socially useful job which is decently paid. (Here I am clearly not referring to those students who are seeking a social revolution by way of a revolution within the University).

There has been a great deal of talk about the abstract and distant nature of the teacher-student relationship, and of the poor quality of many teachers who might, nevertheless, be brilliant academically. I shall not make any general statements on this point. How is it possible to discover the true proportion of good teachers and bad? In the last few weeks, some students from the science faculty have told me about one professor who started the year with 150 students at his lectures and ended up with none. The University in France had one fundamental vice —the absence of any obligation or sanction.

A professor held his chair because of the quality of his work and because he had been co-opted by his colleagues. Once ensconced he could choose to work or not to work, he could concern himself with his students or he could ignore them. Nothing he did could have the slightest effect on his career. I had a colleague at the Sorbonne who had not published anything in twenty years, and who had accomplished the

43

considerable feat of having virtually no students at his lectures. He was a remarkably intelligent man in other ways, but his teaching for various reasons was useless to his students.

{Every professor was supreme master of his chair below God./ An unreasonable professor could paralyse the system; no one could oblige anyone to do anything, the Minister of National Education, the master of hundreds of thousands of civil servants, had no intellectual or pedagogic authority at all. The University, like the rest of French society, lacked intermediate institutions. Not even the dean of the University could force a recalcitrant professor to adopt a reasonable organization of studies in his department. Teaching conditions would be much improved by the creation of intermediate bodies at departmental level with an elected director who, supported by the informal censure of the students and the moral pressure of his colleagues, could exercise a close and legally established watch over what went on./

Were most French professors as authoritarian as they are always claimed to be? Here too it is difficult to make any general statement. In some cases *assistants* and *maîtres-assistants* and students reacted fairly sharply against professors, claiming them to be authoritarians who only occasionally revealed flashes of enlightenment. In most cases American professors use quite a different style; the style of professors in German universities on the other hand used to be far worse than that of their French colleagues. As to the rule of the *mandarins*,[2] this has very different meanings according to whether it is applied to faculties of letters, science, medicine, law or economics. If by the status of mandarin we mean the exercise of arbitrary authority by the head of the group over his colleagues, and his wish to lay down the line of research for his juniors to follow, we find that academics can become mandarins at an early age. I have known colleagues of 40 who are far more mandarins than professors of 60 in the way that they urge everyone working with them to use the same methods, to apply the same techniques, and to produce —as if by chance—the same results. In the disciplines I am familiar with, I have been struck by the stress laid on the intellectual rule of the mandarins, if by this we mean the

44

authoritarianism of the leader of the group in scientific matters. This form of mandarinship is not necessarily as disastrous as it is claimed to be in other disciplines, where the 'old boss' no longer did any work of his own and merely gave his signature to the work of his collaborators. On the other hand a young and talented mandarin can sometimes be a great inspiration.

In the physical and medical sciences, there are serious problems presented by mandarinship which is achieved by the authority of age and rivalry between groups. Knowledge is changing all the time, and a scientist of 25 or 30 may well know more than his older chief. In the United States this problem is solved by selection by merit, the absence of a civil service statute —*statut de la fonction publique*[3]—and by the growing number of laboratories. A university will offer a talented physicist, chemist or medical scientist a laboratory where he can swiftly become the chief; in the United States, however, there are also laboratories where the director is an older man. So everything there depends on the quality of the people involved, and if I may call it that, on their scientific liberalism.

In the faculties of letters, the rule of the mandarins found its particular expression in what I consider to be the excessive influence exerted by the top men, the Sorbonne professors, on the choice of thesis subjects and the nature of the theses. These same 'elders' sometimes also tended to determine the careers of younger men according to the academic or political beliefs they held. This was a deeply ingrained habit which the institution never did enough to oppose.

I would like to say one thing further on this subject. Our present universities house an intellectual lower middle class or semi-proletariat as well as the upper class of the mandarins. In recent years there has been a massive recruitment of *assistants* and *maîtres-assistants* into the faculties of letters, science and law and economics. The former, the *assistants*, are young, *agrégés*, graduates of the *École Normale Supérieur*,[1] who in other times would have been teaching in the *lycées*,[1] but who have found themselves in a far better position than their colleagues who work in schools. These young men are closer to their students, and their political views are often more advanced, but as they will become professors in time, they do not feel themselves to be professional failures and they have no reason to be particularly bitter. But one special category, the *maîtres-assistants*, has arrived in the university world to introduce an element similar to that of the relationship in the *lycées* between *licenciés* or even *certifiés* and *agrégés*.[1] You are aware of the curse of the French University, which is that everyone's career is essentially determined once and for all by the diplomas, titles or grades obtained at the outset of his career. No matter what qualities a *certifié* may have, he will never reach the same level as an *agrégé*. A *licencié* knows as soon as he starts his career the salary he will be earning when he finishes it. This kind of system creates hidden tensions which came to the surface during the period of revolution. Because of the brutal transformation of higher education which has recently taken place, the University is now experiencing contradictions of the same kind. A *maître-assistant* with a 'third-cycle doctorate',[1] not a State doctorate,[1] will probably still be in the same category on a modest salary at the end of his career. His job is not always essentially different from that of a professor or a *chargé d'enseignement*, but he must either limit his ambition once and for all, or get over the next academic hurdle.

According to the law the hierarchy is established by the academic titles obtained at the start of a man's career, and not by his intellectual merit or the effectiveness of his teaching. This system has always seemed to me to be as monstrous as it is difficult to change. I do not think that during all this talk of reforms anyone mentioned the civil service statute, which is supported even by the majority of revolutionary professors. All universities anywhere in the world draw a distinction between different grades of teachers, and there are two ways of doing this. You can either use the French system of degrees and titles, which disgusts me, or you can use a system of promotion by merit, either by co-opting, or based on the judgment of committees of specialists or of the university authorities. I have a feeling that the majority of French teachers might reject the

46

latter system with even greater violence than they criticize our present system. During the events of May, the *assistants*, and sometimes the *maîtres-assistants* or the *chargés d'enseignement* joined in the student movement with much greater enthusiasm than their professors. The *assistants* were moved by various reasons political, professional and by age group solidarity, and the *maîtres-assistants* and the *chargés d'enseignement* joined in for reasons which were both political and professional. So there was a division between young and old—although there were, of course, many exceptions: there were young men who refused to march and old men who insisted on running. Sometimes the existence of this intellectual lower middle class attenuated the clash between professors and students, sometimes it made confusion worse. A professor from a provincial university has told me of *assistants* and *maîtres-assistants* who joined the staff with a 'third-cycle doctorate', who are coming up against the next obstacle—the State doctorate—which they will never obtain, either because they lack the ability, or because they have no time to study. In the universities and the laboratories the class of teachers which is situated between the students and the full professors played a disproportionate part in activism. All the observers of revolutions, Tocqueville, Pareto and the others, know that the most revolutionary elements are not those at the very bottom of the hierarchy but the intermediate elements, which have climbed high enough to be able to see the distance which still lies between them and the summit. Since we are talking about criticisms of professors, I would like to refer to two others which are just as classic.

First complaint: the non-resident professor. There is not the slightest doubt that the professor who does not live in the town where he teaches, and who delivers three hours of lectures in one day, is not doing his job properly. Yet it must be said that the Ministry has fallen into the habit of creating chairs and universities which have no work facilities, no premises and no libraries. There are many teachers who, if they lived in the town where they teach, would have to go to Paris to get access to a laboratory or a library. If the provincial universities are to be transformed into real centres of education and thought, they must be given the necessary facilities.

It is also fashionable to discuss the failings of the *cours magistral*.[1]

Personally I dislike these *cours magistraux*, consisting entirely of lectures, although after some years of experiment, I have limited my teaching at the Sorbonne almost exclusively to this kind of course. The number of students was too great to allow the use of any other method. When I tried to make the students contribute something themselves, to speak to an audience of some 200, they were extremely tense, and their comrades hardly listened to what they had to say—just sat and waited for the professor to start talking again. In the end it was clear that they got more benefit from the *cours magistral* than from this kind of exercise in which after all only a few students could take part, as they did not all get the chance of addressing the group.

I must say, however, that I am absolutely against repeating the same *cours magistral* year after year, with lecture notes which have been stencilled and made available to readers. This is current practice in some faculties, but I consider it entirely unjustifiable, although there may be an excuse for it when professors offer ideas or facts which cannot be found in books, at least not in the same form. I do not think that I have ever repeated the same course twice. I may be right or wrong not to have done so, of course, but I would be bored myself by repeating the same course. Moreover, I have never understood why, once a course of lectures has been stencilled, the professor does not merely hand it over to the students and spend his time in developing parts of it, or commenting on a chapter, or going into more detailed explanation.

Of course, even an original *cours magistral* has its drawbacks; on the other hand for students, all of whom know very little, to form groups to teach themselves, does not seem to me the most effective of teaching methods. (When former students have told me of their clearest memories of their time at the Sorbonne, they have referred most often to some *cours magistral* or other. Some had enjoyed a one-year course I delivered on Montesquieu, and others said that they had appreciated my critique of Sartre's *Dialectical Reason*.) I have rung the changes on *cours magistraux* for ten years, but in most cases the discussion groups of students which we have tried to organize many times at the Sorbonne have broken up after a few months. The students did not always feel that they were learning anything from each other. It is true, of course, that there are occasions when students can derive mutual benefit from discussion, but there is a real danger that reciprocal education may degenerate into a political discussion group. I do not think that the traditional methods are beyond reproach, but I would not condemn them out of hand.

Perhaps for the sake of completeness I should introduce one final subject, which has been raised many times—the Fouchet-Aigrain reform.

Academics are divided as to the merits and failings of this reform, but in my opinion the Ministry of Education, against the advice of teachers, committed one unforgivable blunder in deciding to apply it to students who had begun their studies under the old system. This decision led to trouble and protest almost everywhere, protests which were largely justified, and could have been avoided. The simultaneous organization of courses of study under both the new régime and the old posed almost inextricable problems, and really had a traumatic effect on some students. The dean of every university in the country had pointed out this mistake in advance, and in this case, for once, we know where the responsibility lies. The reform, para-doxically, and contrary to all the current educational theories, at least in the humanities, exaggerated the separation between faculties and made it much more difficult for a student to move from one department to another. For example, a *licencié* in psychology lost his right to work towards a master's degree in sociology. So here we come up against a further absurdity. We now have to ask whether a candidate has the necessary paper qualification instead of trying to establish whether he has the ability to undertake a particular course of studies successfully.

A.D.   Just listening to you, I get a very clear impression that there is a great need for change but also a very limited capacity to absorb innovation. I get the impression that whatever the merits and the shortcomings of the French University may be, it needs channels leading from one form of education to another, and right through to the top, or from one type of teacher to another, and perhaps from student to teacher.

R.A.   Throughout the world all universities tend towards conservatism. They tend to conserve because their function is to hand on to their students not only knowledge, but also an idea of an ideal human being. And for rather more profound reasons, which Durkheim[4] has discussed, they tend to close in on themselves, and to be content with a traditional organization based on values which they justly still hold to. I was talking recently with one of the leading reformers of the American University, a former President of the University of California. He has made an enormous contribution to the expansion of that university, which has now become a 'mass university' and has experienced a revolt of 'student-rats' suffering from over-population. He told me that every time he had set up a new campus with new forms of organization, he had noticed at the end of a few years that once the institution had settled down it was just as resistant to reforms as were older establishments. Perhaps the only way that the University will ever be able to transform itself is by a process of constantly splitting up into new organisms. In Britain the new universities are introducing innovations.

Let us consider the case of grades or diplomas. I am opposed personally to national competitive examinations—at least to the majority of those I know—and I have often criticized the *agrégations*, which do not provide any reliable measure either of academic ability or teaching ability. I am not even in favour of the State doctorate thesis, a major work done prematurely at the start of a man's academic career. But those people who urge that these things should be eliminated are not always aware of the administrative difficulties.

Suppose for instance that it was decided to force all secondary school teachers to teach the same time-table, and to pay them all the same salary, no matter what their qualifications were. The administrators tell me that if this were done, the civil service unions would all demand that everybody must work to the *agrégé*'s time-table and receive an *agrégé*'s salary. And would it indeed be equitable to remove the advantages to which they are entitled by the civil service statute from people who enjoy what we term the 'privileges of *agrégation*'?

A.D.   In a way this is the same problem as that of the Fouchet-Aigrain reform, a matter of transition.

R.A.   Indeed it is. But it could not be solved in two years, as the Fouchet-Aigrain reform would have been. This would be a matter of years or decades. Today's *agrégés* will retain the status to which they are entitled to the end of their lives. They will keep their time-table, and they will keep their incremental scale which will carry them up to a certain salary. Then again, if you put *certifiés* and *agrégés* on the same level, would you put *licenciés* on a par with *certifiés*? If time-tables and salaries were levelled off for all secondary school teachers, would we be able to get by without some other form of selection? I doubt whether, in the French system at least, one could go as far as putting every one on the same level, because this reform would mean that every-one would acquire privileges, and not that some few would lose their privileges in the general good. Of course many tensions, injustices, vipers' nests are created in the *lycées* by the distinc-tions between four or five different categories who will remain separated as long as they live by virtue of qualifications they acquired up to thirty years earlier. If, however, the French people do not want promotion by merit, if the risk entailed in this kind of promotion is more than they will accept, then they con-demn themselves to be governed by abstract, anonymous regula-tions. Now the French being what they have always been, which do they dislike more? The vipers' nest which results from the existence of separate categories determined by qualifications obtained right at the start of their careers, or the risk entailed in a system of promotion by merit? Or, would they prefer to be levelled off at an average point or at a lower point? Those are some of the administrative problems which no one discussed in the reform commissions, and which the Ministry is considering today.

As far as higher education is concerned, must we reduce all categories to the same level? Certainly not. How should distinctions be established? Do we abolish national competitions? All right.

The formula which seems to have the support of most reformers involves the ending of the *agrégation*, and perhaps of the State doctorate. In this case the 'third-cycle' doctorate would become the equivalent of a Ph.D. or the *Habilitationsschrift*. A list of those fitted to teach in institutions of higher education, which would, of course, be a very long list, would be drawn up at national level. Provincial universities will recruit their staff very often on local considerations, which will not necessarily raise the standard but which will entail the regionalization of recruitment, with the consequence that there will be some reduction in tension and rivalry. But the 'third-cycle' doctorate has been devalued at a great rate!

A.D.   Now perhaps we could talk about the revolution.

R.A.   The revolution had a dual character. Its primary objective was the establishment of student power in the University, and then for a few days it aimed at bringing about a political revolution through the student youth. Simultaneously, the University revolution was directed towards achieving a transformation of the structure of the University for its own sake, and with no reference to any political or social revolution. Let us examine this strange revolution and its double target of student power and political subversion.

We have discovered that there was a small group of revolutionary students and teachers on the left of the Communist Party. (The Communists themselves were fairly moderate inside the University as well as outside.) Some of the members of this small group were associated with the P.S.U., others to Marxist-Leninist youth movements, Trotskyites or Maoists, whom we can lump together as revolutionaries or *enragés*—extremists. Some of these were inclined to anarchism, some to Castroism. They started the movement off first at Nanterre and then at the Sorbonne, and then from Monday 13th they provoked the occupation of the Sorbonne and set up a kind of Student

Commune. This was followed almost immediately by what some call the abdication and the capitulation of the university authorities, and which others see as the solidarity of a number of the teachers with their students. Everyone must make his own judgment as to which of the two it was.

The revolutionary psychodrama was obsessed throughout by precedents. When the professorial assembly of the Sorbonne decided to hand over its powers, or to hand over the power to draw up reforms to a plenary assembly which would include teachers of all grades, one professor suddenly and spontaneously evoked a great event from the past; 'My dear colleagues, it is the night of the 4th August'.[5]

Although this might offend some people, I must say again that I think this reference to the night of 4th August was ridiculous. If the analogy must be drawn, the wearers of gowns would only really have been imitating the wearers of wigs if they had solemnly decreed that from henceforth there would be only one category of teacher and that all would be paid the same. To hand over the powers of the professorial assembly to a plenary assembly was merely to exaggerate the shortcomings of the old system to a ridiculous degree. An assembly of 100 to 150 professors is incapable of serious discussion. The same applies *a fortiori* to a plenary assembly of several hundred people, some of whom are using revolutionary action techniques.

The very idea that the professors were privileged needs some comment. If a professor has any control over his students, he must not abandon an authority which merely constitutes the exercise of a necessary function. A journalist on *L'Humanité*[1] wrote recently that the teacher-student relationship is necessarily unequal. A professor would have to be very ignorant indeed to be more ignorant than his students, particularly in their first years at university. Of course the same is far from true in a research laboratory where young scientists of 25 work side by side with scientists of 60. In this case inequality is far from necessary. In the university reforms as applied to faculties of letters or of sciences, however, power was being handed over either to plenary assemblies (of teachers) which were too big to allow

53

sensible discussion, or to general assemblies which included an indeterminate number of students. The students who took part in the general assemblies belonged to the activist minorities. All these assemblies were illegal, and professors or deans who recognized them as having a legal status were themselves breaking the law, and were consequently behaving like revolutionaries.

The term 'revolutionary' should not be taken as pejorative. Quite the opposite. Anyone in France today who is not a revolutionary, or who says he is not, is regarded with suspicion. I must say that I was unaware of the number of unsuspected revolutionaries among my colleagues. I did not think that professors of constitutional law would come to the point of developing a juridical theory of the revolutionary phenomenon. I did not know that so many of my colleagues who had been cool towards my suggested reforms would suddenly speed past me of their own free will and endorse with evident and apparently sincere enthusiasm changes for which they had never had the slightest sympathy in the past.

Did the professors suddenly see the light? Did they abdicate their powers because of their own guilty consciences? Did anxiety sweep away their doubts? Let us leave everyone free to answer these questions as they think fit, and merely accept the fact that the authorities tolerated the establishment of plenary assemblies and general assemblies for which there was no provision in the law of the land nor in the regulations of the University. Many professors recognized these *ad hoc* assemblies as having a legal status, and not merely as commissions to examine possible reforms. Several faculties (I will name no names and wish to accuse no-one) in effect accepted this quasi-revolutionary legality. Professorial assemblies dissolved themselves of their own accord and handed over their powers to improvised assemblies. The result of this upheaval is a strange, unprecedented situation. Can the ministry ignore a *fait accompli*? Can those professors who accepted these insurrectional transformations, apparently of their own free will, come back on the agreement they gave? Can they plead that they acted under duress? How can the former legality be restored so that new structures can be properly introduced?

The attempt to turn the university revolution into a social and political revolution was at its peak in the six-day period between the speech of 24th May and the speech of 30th May. The students sent delegations into the factories, which were being picketed by the Communists. The U.N.E.F. tried to overtake the Communist Party on its left and to put the theory of a social revolution proceeding from a university revolution into practice. Maybe some young workers had a feeling of solidarity with the students, but the workers and the Communist Party were well aware of the difference between the relative situations of workers and students. Will you allow me to make a remark of good sense, but in bad taste: who earn their living in the University? the teachers. The students are acquiring an education with the intention of getting diplomas which will subsequently assure them of a social position better than that which a worker can usually hope for. The confusion of student power and the power of the workers makes sense only in the jargon of revolution. There is some sense to be seen in the participation of workers' representatives in the management of a factory, and similarly in the participation of students or their representatives in some aspects of the running of a university. But no State worthy of the name would hand over the management of the universities to those who—far from earning their living in them —are being instructed free of charge so that later they will be able to get a well-paid job. The French State is not the only one to provide free higher education, but its payment of family allowances contributes towards the growing number of students in the faculties. It encourages the middle-class families, which still provide the majority of students, to go on sending their sons and daughters to university. Student power, the power of those who are getting a free education over those who earn their living by teaching, would put the seal of approval on the authority of the ignorant, and who admit their ignorance by their very presence at an educational establishment.

On the other hand, if the aim of student power is to turn the

University into a political institution and to use this as a means to throw society into turmoil, everything is clear. In that case we are dealing with a weapon of war to destroy the University as a place of learning, and to attack the social order as a whole by means of its destruction. We shall have to see whether even a liberal State will take liberalism as far as tolerating such an exercise from its civil servants. The only universities which have any experience of this kind of contest are a handful in Latin America, and they have also experienced the inevitable consequences of this kind of action.

The University charter gave all teachers a right to complete freedom of opinion, and even freedom of political commitment outside the University. Inside the University, teachers undertook to maintain neutrality and to observe professional values. I am of course aware of the gap which existed between the charter and reality. When I was elected to the Sorbonne, I doubt whether many of my Communist colleagues voted for me, although I know that I had the support of several professors from the Left. In some circumstances political considerations were borne in mind when people were being co-opted to posts, and some professors selected their *assistants* because of their political views. I was an extreme case because of my activities outside the University, and at all events, my colleagues quite explicitly refuse to let political motives be seen during an election. This hypocrisy places an effective limit on the part which politics could play in the University. If political motivation was camouflaged, it was held within certain bounds. Today's fashionable theories demand that the camouflage should be ripped off political motivation because of the ideological implications of any kind of education.

I agree that even the teaching of the history of art could reveal some vague political implications if one looked hard enough for them. There are always political implications in the teaching of sociology, without any doubt at all. But everyone is perfectly well aware of the difference between *exposing* all the various doctrines as objectively as possible, and setting out the arguments for and against them, and *imposing* one single doctrine

56

and rejecting all the others. Up to now the overwhelming majority of teachers have observed this distinction, and from now on a small number will refuse to do so. We are probably all guilty of partiality in our various ways, but as long as everyone was in agreement about the need to observe the ethic of the liberal university, almost everyone felt obliged to resist temptations towards partiality. If teachers ever subscribe to the idea that the University should be a political instrument, impartiality will go by the board and the University will die. In liberal countries the University can exist only if it observes the moral code of liberalism. In the socialist countries of eastern Europe, indeed, the universities are losing more and more of their political coloration; politics have been almost entirely rooted out of the teaching of natural sciences, physics, mathematics and biology. Stalinism is a thing of the past, and Einstein or genetic theory are no longer connected with dialectical materialism; no one would now have the temerity to condemn the theory of relativity on idealistic grounds, nor to attack genetics as a bourgeois science. Even in the social sciences, where Marxism is still a compulsory subject, the spirit of objective study and reasoned controversy is making headway. I have met many colleagues from Poland, Czechoslovakia and the Soviet Union who have read my books and who discussed them exactly as my French colleagues do. They rejected my conclusions while accepting some of my arguments or factual statements. It was perfectly possible to engage with them in a reasoned discussion of doctrines which are loaded with political implications. The tendency we can see in France today is in the opposite direction, towards the replacement of reasoned discussion of political subjects by the kind of argument which is used at public meetings. This moral degradation is a national catastrophe.

A.D.   You have pointed out what you see as the negative aspects of student power. One might ask now whether it has any positive sides.

R.A.   Most of the discussions and proposals which I have been able to find out about deal with what I shall call Constitutions of the University. Here we can see yet another instance of

powerful influence of traditional models on the collective unconscious mind. No sooner have the students got a revolution
half begun than they start working out Constitutions. Students
of the *Institut d'études politiques* spent several weeks drafting a
Constitution, and when the document finally appeared it was
quite clear that the reformers had been unable to think up a
single new idea about the content or the method of education.
The proposals in this Constitution are simply re-hashes of ideas
which have been put forward time and again over the past few
years. There are some exceptions: medical students, and students
from the *Écoles des Mines*[1] and the *Beaux-Arts*[1] proposed substantial changes. Students are exactly like their elders in the
way that as soon as they have grasped some ill-defined power,
they try to stabilize it by setting it out in writing.

It is pointless to discuss the particular details of a constitutional organization unless one knows the nature, the aim, the
limits of the powers under consideration. The constitutions of a
department for first-year students, of a faculty of 5,000 students,
of a faculty of 50,000, or of a laboratory with a staff of 500 must
necessarily be different one from another. The ways in which
students can participate will vary in each case. The student
power of freshmen in a sociology department has nothing in
common with that of research workers in a laboratory where
young scientists are working under the direction of an old chief.
My criticism of the majority of the documents produced by the
reform commissions is that they all gave pride of place to the
legal or constitutional aspects of what they were trying to do.

The present turmoil will give birth to some irreversible reforms which will probably be a disappointment to their
initiators.

In the first place we have the departments, such as the departments of sociology, classics or history. Here it has been agreed
that the students will be represented on the departmental
management committees. I have some reservations about the
idea of equal representation, as I think there is a danger in the
symbolism it embodies. The aim of equal representation is
essentially to overcome the inequality which is an intrinsic part

of the teacher-student relationship. This is not to say that the teachers are superior in terms of dignity or of intelligence (there are stupid teachers and intelligent students) and they are certainly not superior by definition; by definition it is the students who will have the last word. But quite simply the teaching relationship loses all meaning as soon as anyone postulates the equality of knowledge. Even this point is not vital, for if the students are reasonable, it makes no difference whether the commissions are on an equal representation basis or not. If the commissions have to take decisions by vote, they will not be able to operate in any case. So I accept management committees elected by the various types of members of the University, but I would stipulate one fundamental principle: the managing professors must be elected by their peers and not by a students or mixed assemblies. Election by mixed assemblies, which the jargon calls '*mixité*', introduces a danger of demagogy and of an unacceptable degree of politics coming into the voting. A professor whose political ideas are distasteful to the students might find himself removed from the management bodies. There is some difficulty too in the election of teachers; will the teachers' representatives be elected by a single college composed of all the teachers from the top of the scale down to the bottom? As there are far more *assistants* and *maîtres-assistants* than there are professors, there would be a risk that an all-embracing electoral college might also become dangerously demagogic. It seems to me that three separate colleges would be needed, not to protect privileges, but to ensure the smooth running of the university institutions. It is not enough to abdicate one's responsibilities to prove that one is a good democrat.

At faculty level, everything depends on the degree of autonomy. Everyone seems to agree that the faculties should have a certain amount of freedom in the allocation of funds provided by government. The professorial assemblies were too large to carry out management functions efficiently, and seemed to keep going round in circles; mixed student-teacher assemblies would be still larger. Would they be more open to outside views? I am personally very willing to consider projects designed to open the universities to representatives of economic and social groups from outside. What management requires, are small committees not exclusively composed of teachers and students.

It all depends on what you are trying to manage. For the moment, in the faculties of letters, the finances are mainly absorbed in paying the wages of the teaching staff. These funds are in a sense allocated in advance under the civil service statute. If the civil service statute is not altered, the percentage of these funds remaining to be administered by the faculty will be fairly small. Running costs, on the other hand, can be quite substantial in a science faculty with laboratories. Altogether it seems unavoidable that the financial machinery should be on the following pattern: the budget for higher education as a whole would be voted by the National Assembly. The University, taken as a whole, is at the service of the nation, and the representatives of the whole nation could decide on the total allocation of funds available for the education of the young.

Will the division of funds between the various universities or regions be made by Parliament? I think so. (Note—the law setting down general principles has decided otherwise. R.A.) The autonomy of the University would begin to play a rôle when we come to the question of the distribution of funds between the various faculties and departments. Each faculty would have to decide on the way the money was divided between its various departments. At this point the political infighting between various pressure groups would begin. The various disciplines would exert the same kind of pressure within the university assemblies as pressure groups in the National Assembly use to try to get their allocations increased. Will all this lead to a fairer distribution of funds? I doubt it, but as everyone seems to want to see the introduction of university parliaments, very well. At least let us avoid government by assembly, and let us have small management committees.

I will go along with the experiment. I am afraid that the students will be disappointed when they come to exercise the power they have won for themselves, and that they will discover just how frustrating and time-wasting assemblies can be. The students will lose their illusions and they will recognize the faults in the Constitutions they have drafted. Management and co-management of faculties have been confused far too often with the valid demand for better contact between students and teachers and with the need for that contact to be placed on a permanent footing, so that teachers know what the students have absorbed and what they have not, and what they want and what they do not want. Students who demand participation in management bodies have got the most extraordinary illusions about the pleasure and profit they will derive from this exercise, as long as participation manages to avoid being a political weapon. The power of distributing limited funds between teaching and research will bring little joy either to the faculties or to the *Centre National de Recherche Scientifique*.[6] It will merely be a thankless experiment in political education. Universities, like industrial firms, have to satisfy the demands of efficiency and be subject to a restrictive discipline which is a combination of rationality and scarcity.

The discipline of rationality: the limited funds available must be used as efficiently as possible. Efficiency can be defined in many ways: we can have efficiency directed towards specific aims in learning or research; and we can have efficiency with regard to professional training. And immediately we go off into areas of prolonged controversy.

The constraints of scarcity: most teachers and the whole of the student movement reject the principle of selection. Now all that selection means is that the State is not prepared to provide unlimited funds to give any boy or girl free access to the universities. In the United States higher education has to be paid for (at least nominally), and there are generous scholarship awards, a system which is far preferable to the French free system. It seems that democracy demands that the children of the 'P.D.G.'s'[7]—the rich—should be given higher education for nothing. My conception of democracy is rather different. Can the principle of free university education be revised? I hope it can, but I doubt it. On the other hand the State will not provide funds to cope with an unlimited number of students.

If all the students who entered the universities completed their courses, a university degree, which even today has comparatively little importance to an employer, would have none at all. The fact that anyone who has passed the *baccalauréat* can automatically go on to university creates an increased pressure of scarcity on the management bodies, and forces the teachers to exercise selection by increasing the percentage of examination failures.

The tense relations between students and teachers are due in part to the fact that university teachers in France have to use annual examinations as their method of selection. In England and the Soviet Union the selection is made before admission, although the methods used are different. Selection before admission relieves university teachers of having to exercise selection by means of failing people in examinations.

In the Sovet Union selection for university admission is very stiff indeed. But there are a large number of vocational centres where students who do not get into university can be trained for a career. I am in favour of a system of this kind, because even in a liberal country and perhaps there more than anywhere else, it is the only way of saving the liberal University. I have heard it objected that this system would lead to university entrance being open only to members of the privileged classes. In fact our present system leads to the same result as well as having other regrettable consequences. For the moment I stress that selection of students before admission would lead to better relations between teachers and students, and would eliminate the overcrowding in the first year, the overpopulation neurosis, and the traumatic effect of the examination threat; it would make it possible to achieve a reasonable balance between resources, premises, funds available, teachers and the number of students. I hope that the Government will take advantage of the autonomy of the universities, which has the support of all students, to introduce the principle of selection, which they all oppose. If they sit on management committees, they will gradually come to realize the double constraints of maintaining a rational course of study in conditions of scarcity. They will have to compare a number x of students with an amount y of resources; they will then either have to accept a disproportion between the resources and the number of students, or they will have to agree to pre-selection, or entrust the teachers with making a selection at the end of the year. In criticizing the situation, they will have realized why the teachers bear so much ill will, what the effects are of the constraints from which all institutions in modern societies suffer. Large universities are typical; the drawing up of constitutions, and the acceptance of participation will not by themselves solve the fundamental problems which the French University faces today.

For a start, how can we eliminate the quarrels which reign within the University? How can we re-establish a minimum of unity and sense of community between colleagues who judge each other so harshly? How can we stop being political enemies and become colleagues again? How can we come to accept that *assistants* whom we appointed in ignorance of their political opinions have suddenly discovered a vocation not merely for university revolution—which is bad enough—but for political revolution? I have no illusions. Politics has got into the French University, and will be there for many years to come. The abcess will have to be allowed to heal gradually, and tolerable relationships between colleagues will have to be re-established. But I have written recently, and I still believe, that the French University is more deeply divided today than it has ever been since it was reconstituted at the end of the last century. How can we treat as colleagues, men who thought it right to mobilize boys of 14 or 15 and send them on to the barricades? or indoctrinate them to take part in a political adventure? A great gulf has opened between men who consider it compatible with the moral function of a teacher to mobilize, to indoctrinate, and to establish cells, and liberal academics like myself. It is a gulf which cannot be bridged in the near future. The University rested on a moral code which has been violated, of ten in good faith, in the sense that those who violated it no longer accepted its validity, but those who still do accept it can no longer keep up the hypocritical charade of politeness as if nothing had happened.

The first problem cannot be solved until years of open or concealed conflicts have passed. There will probably be new student outbursts, and certain types of teachers will probably engage in varying degrees of subversion. This problem cannot be solved by the Government; indeed no one can solve it by a wave of a magic wand. If we want to see the survival of the French universities, we must continue to oppose 'critical universities' or 'revolutionary universities', which are not universities at all, but merely the tools of revolution. Then we must try gradually, first in the science faculties, then in medicine, in political economy, in law and finally in the faculties of letters, to bring back the majority of the teachers to an awareness of a moral code, and to persuade them that there is a limit to the rôle of politics in the University. Of course, by speaking of the elimination of politics, I do not mean that the students should be forbidden to hold political meetings on university premises. I mean that there should be no intrusion of political and ideological debate into courses or seminars where teachers and students should be engaged in a serious consideration of public affairs.

Problem number two is to find some way of bringing the number of students into line with the resources available. The worst possible solution would be to maintain the present disproportion between the number of students accepted and the resources of premises, staff and funds which the nation is prepared to provide for higher education. The French University will hang between life and death until this disproportion is eliminated.

There is one special problem—the cancer of Paris. As long as the monstrous University of Paris continues to exist—and it may even double in size, given the rôle of Paris in French life—we shall always be at the mercy of an explosion in the capital spreading to the provinces. The problem has no short-term solution unless some established rights are withdrawn,—for instance the right of every holder of the *baccalauréat* to enter any university department of his choice, in any university they choose, or in the university in the town where they live. Every other country has accepted the principle that students must be prepared to move

64

away from home. This principle should be introduced in France, but today, France is the only country which does not have this mobility or is not considering introducing it. A better distribution of students among cities and academic departments would be at least a genuine if modest contribution to the necessary task of reducing the crowds of students in Paris. The University of Paris contributes to making the capital so monstrous! When Paris has a fever, France trembles; until the University of Paris is broken up, nothing can be put right.

Fourthly, we should see some progress in the development of teacher-student relations. The events of May will probably play their part in this process, provided that the *enragés* do not manage to turn the new institutions away from their new functions, and if the new institutions are run in the spirit of the reform and not in a spirit of revolution. Given even this optimistic hypothesis we must not conceal the dangers. Even the moderate students more or less believe in student power. Their argument goes as far as challenging the authority of the teacher as such. In certain cases this challenge is justified, but if this view is allowed to become general, there is a real risk that it will provoke a backlash from the teachers, particularly from the best ones: if the students think they know all the answers, let them look after themselves. It happens that employers meet a strike with a lock-out; the reaction of teachers to agitation and 'politicizing' may come one day as a surprise to even the best students.

In fifth place we come to a fundamental problem: as the number of students grows, they will not all be able to find jobs in teaching. There must therefore be an increase in the number of other institutions of higher education with a practical bias (a massive programme of development of university institutes of technology), while the education offered in the faculties of science and letters must gradually be restructured into something other than its traditional form. In other words, the numbers of students of psychology or sociology, of English or history, should be kept in proportion with the number of probable career possibilities. Revolutionary jargon calls this process the 'technocratic recovery' of the May revolution. This technocratic recovery is merely the triumph of common sense over ideology, demagogy, or subversive intent.

The technocratic recovery consists of preparing young people for the professions they intend to follow. Of course there can be no constant ratio between the number of young people who have acquired a certain class of diploma and the jobs available. Higher education is an advantage in its own right. As the general level of education rises, the same jobs are done by men who have been better educated. The illusion that a diploma is a guarantee of a job, and a job of a particular kind, is becoming absurd. But it makes sense at the present time not to make frustration worse by giving young people diplomas which will not in fact help them to find a job. The technocratic recovery, which I call the adaptation of education to possible careers, is in the interests of everyone, and is in danger of rejection by everyone. It will be rejected by the defenders of the traditional University, who say that culture is an end in itself, above, beyond and incidental to any profession. It will be rejected by the revolutionaries who will accuse the technocrats of acting to save the bourgeois capitalist society, although socialist technocrats act in exactly the same way. It will be rejected by the fanatics of democratization who will accuse the technocrats of pushing the children of the lower classes towards inferior jobs. All these ideologies— general culture, the revolution, democratization, will come together to prolong and aggravate the crisis of career outlets, and to maintain a situation which any local student disturbance could spark off. I hope that there are enough teachers, students and administrators with enough common sense to comprehend the problem and able to carry out the gradual process of adapting courses, even maybe adapting whole faculties, to the needs of vocational or professional education. If this adaptation is rejected, the only alternative is a massive reduction in the number of students in the University, and a vast increase in the numbers in the Engineering Schools or the Institutes of Technology. If the University is not a preparation for anything, it must be reserved for a minority; if it is to be open to a larger number, it must prepare them for more than reading Vergil with the aid of a dictionary.

Now we come to the last of the major problems, the problem of degrees and university competitive examinations. I have pointed out one major drawback of these competitive examinations: they impose uniformity on all universities. Again, these examinations fix salary scales once and for all, and they have a traumatic effect on many young people as well as on many older people. I have always been, and I am still, opposed to these competitive examinations. I do not claim to have a well-considered view on the medical *internat* examination, although it seems to me that memory, and the accumulation of facts which may turn up in the examination plays a very large part in this kind of competition. I do know something about the *agrégations*, and here I deplore the importance of rhetoric. Rhetoric is no guarantee of scientific knowledge, nor of an aptitude for teaching. I would prefer to see an extended teacher-training for potential secondary school teachers, and a scientific education for those who are going into research. I have other objections to this kind of competitive examination, to the *agrégations* in law, in political economy, and in philosophy, which give an advantage to a certain kind of mind, and to a certain extent to a particular social class. Unfortunately any protest against examinations and competitions always leads to the rejection of any kind of discrimination. French culture is a combination of a strict hierarchy with a longing for equality. The University is a microcosm of French society, and reflects its contradictions; a hierarchy established by university degrees, which is accepted with a clear conscience in as much as it corresponds to merit assessed by an anonymous competition. This clear conscience has now been clouded by various objections: there is no guarantee of the fairness of these competitive examinations. Some favour candidates from certain social classes, and these degrees or titles, the *agrégation* especially, form a kind of class distinction within the University in much the same way as for many years the *baccalauréat* constituted a kind of social barrier. The sociologists have managed to give the academics a bad conscience by showing them that their reconciliation of the egalitarian ideal with a hierarchy based on anonymous competitions was unrealistic and illusory, for two reasons: the fact that examiners may not always be right, and the doubts that have been cast on the qualities which are needed for success in these competitive examinations. These criticisms seem to me to be largely justified. In effect, the reconciliation of the egalitarian ideal and the existence of the hierarchy is very far from perfect, and the university meritocracy certainly very imperfect. (All meritocracies can be criticized.)

Unfortunately, even if we were able to get rid of this system, what could replace it apart from either the total abolition of all discrimination, or the introduction of promotion by merit assessed by a panel of competent and honest judges? In the United States, competition between universities of varying prestige which offer different salaries, and which create laboratories for talented young scientists, makes it possible to avoid a hierarchy of degrees and titles. But in France?

Before we end this conversation, I would like to say something about the fashionable subject of democratization. This word can have three meanings when it is applied to the University.

First, it can envisage the redistribution of the authority of management within departments, faculties and universities. The participation of students in the organization of studies, or of teachers in the distribution of funds, is the equivalent of a new relationship between students and teachers or between teachers and the Ministry of National Education (or between the central administration and the regional agencies). I have already talked about this. As regards the democratization of the teacher-student relationship, or of the form that this relationship takes, this depends above all on the number of students in the classrooms, and the way they behave.

In a second sense, democratization is used to mean an increase in the number of students who come from working class or peasant backgrounds. Sociologists in every country have known for a long time that selection for education is also to a certain extent a social selection. They have identified many reasons for the inequality of children in a system based on the theory of equality. There is the influence of the social class of the family on school results; there is the question as to what extent the culture the child receives in the home is related to academic culture; there is the part played by the knowledge that the child acquires in the home, and the fact that the amount of this knowledge varies according to social class; there is the point that schools in the country and in small towns may be of poorer quality, and that parents and children from the lower classes are less interested in school work and more concerned about the need for the child to start earning a wage, and so on.

Pierre Bourdieu, whose book *les Héritiers* (*The Inheritors*) was read and probably misunderstood by the students, has turned up facts in the case of France which are duplicated to a greater or less degree in all societies, even, as far as we can tell, in socialist societies (although probably the phenomenon is less significant there). Bourdieu has produced a very delicate analysis of socio-educational mechanisms, but at the same time he has been very careful to present facts, which of themselves cannot be disputed, in such a way as to make it possible to derive a political and ideological interpretation from them.

He has given the idea of inheritors a pejorative turn, as if the handing down of intellectual values within the family is to be condemned because it makes it impossible to ensure that all children start life on an equal basis. He suggests, though he does not state, that a different form of teaching would make it possible to eliminate educational inequalities which can be attributed to social inequalities, and has also suggested that reformers should make their first priority the reduction of social handicaps —which is a perfectly legitimate opinion to hold, but not a scientific truth. In the end he leaves his readers to choose between two interpretations of his criticism of the universities: does he want everyone to be given access to academic culture, or does he condemn this culture itself, at least in the form which it is given in the traditional universities by 'charismatic' teachers (among whom Bourdieu is certainly an outstanding figure)?

This open choice, whether it was intended or not, made his views acceptable both to men of the left and to scientists, the latter being attracted by the quality of his analyses, and the former by the revolutionary implications they can find in these analyses, both for teaching methods—for which a change is as desirable as it will be difficult to accomplish—as well as for the University and society.

Is it desirable that more children of workers and peasants should swell the ranks of the students? There can hardly be any discussion about the desirability of the aim, but it is not easy to think of methods of achieving it, nor of how to apply them once found. Is it desirable that the University should change the nature of the culture which it transmits? In one sense this culture is in a constant state of self renewal, as knowledge increases and societies change. Should the process of renewal be speeded up? Maybe. But the idea of the democratization of culture conceals a conception which is entirely alien to Pierre Bourdieu, the conception of a popular or Marxist culture which would be of more value than academic or bourgeois culture.

This is an instance of the difficulties of achieving objectivity in sociology. Well-supported facts are used to bolster up an ideology or a demagogy simply by omission of other facts which are equally well established: the inequality of the abilities transmitted genetically, the varying success in school of children from the same bourgeois background, the social mobility which even the conservative university is gradually beginning to promote, and the impossibility of there ever being complete equality at the start. Society, any society, makes a selection between individuals as social beings, not as individuals reduced to what they would be if the influence of their family background were expunged. Moreover a society in which the prospect of promotion seemed to each and everyone to be limitless would entail ferocious competition and might result in still more painful tensions. In France as she is today, an increase in the non-bourgeois elements in the student population would probably be in the collective interest and would certainly coincide with most Frenchmen's idea of justice.

The May revolution was nurtured on this ideology debased into facile demagogy but it did nothing to help solve the problem.

The lesson to be drawn from *The Inheritors* does not seem to me (until I am proved wrong) to be that we should set about indoctrinating the workers in 'critical universities'; that would be much more an exploit of actual inheritors gripped by the charisma of ideology!

3

The Death and Resurrection
of Gaullism

A.D. To begin our conversation on political problems, and on the key problem of Gaullism in particular, I think that there is at least a seeming paradox which was clear to everyone in the way in which Gaullism changed in an extraordinarily short time from being something which was responsible for the crisis, something which at all events was seriously threatened, into something which suddenly reappeared triumphant.

R.A. There is an obvious and indisputable contrast: but I do not find it paradoxical or surprising. You are aware of my excessive predilection for historical parallels: every revolutionary crisis in France in the nineteenth century, once it had passed through the stage of barricades or 'lyrical illusions,' was followed by a return to power of the party which represented order. Louis Philippe was overthrown by a riot in Paris in February 1848. In April, elections held with universal suffrage gave an enormous majority to the party of order, which included many Orleanists. I am one of those who have long thought that the major weakness of all monarchies in the first part of the nineteenth century was that they all rejected something which could have saved them—universal suffrage. Universal suffrage usually turns out to be a conservative force. The selective suffrage which operated in France in the last century was full of contradictions; legitimists and orleanists, republicans and bonapartists were much more violently opposed to each other in the privileged classes from which the electorate was drawn than in the masses, who were essentially prepared to accept stable government provided that the social gains of the great revolution were left intact. If Louis Philippe had turned to the vote of the people and had found a Massu[1] to defend the Tuileries, he might have got the same kind of majority after the February riots as General de Gaulle got in June after the May riots. What is paradoxical about the present crisis is that a régime which was almost overthrown by street movements gained subsequently when the tide turned. So we may hope that France will not suffer the equivalent of the days of June or 'Versailles' exploits.[2] So the development of this French revolutionary crisis is in line with historical precedents, with the reservation that as the Sovereign owed at least part of his legitimacy to universal suffrage, and having resisted subversion, was able to benefit from the conservative reaction of the French people.

We can add, if you like, an explanation drawn from sociological analysis. The street demonstrations and riots were the work of active minorities. In some circumstances these minorities succeeded in involving the semi-passive mass. For a few days or a few weeks a growing number of Frenchmen dreamt of changing the world. If the active minorities had taken power, this illusion might have lasted a few months or even, possibly, a few years instead of a few days. But when the French went to the polls in June, they had the feeling of having been spectators of some extraordinary and absurd performance—a carnival, saturnalia or a nihilist revolution, I don't know which. Everything had been turned upside down. There had been no reforms. The French economy had been pushed into inflation. The Common Market had been compromised. No-one knew what the aims of the revolutionaries had been. How can one be surprised that the average Frenchman voted for those who, even if they had been responsible for the previous crisis, seemed to be the only ones capable of controlling its consequences? The May

73

revolution in the University was directed more against the University itself than against General de Gaulle. When the strikes turned into a general strike, this was aimed more against society than against General de Gaulle in person, although he was also a target. In other words, the May movement had such vague aims, ideologies and ambitions that after the event many Frenchmen might have thought, rightly or wrongly, that the Bastille which the May revolutionaries sought to overthrow was not a man, not institutions, but a metaphysical entity which has been christened 'the consumer society'—which gave André Malraux with his taste for brilliant, albeit shallow epigrams, the opportunity of proclaiming that General de Gaulle, although politically irreproachable, could do nothing when faced with a revolt which was part of universal history. On this point, Malraux is in agreement with Trotskyites or anarchists like Morin, Lefort or Coudray.

A.D.   You have used two expressions 'barricades' and 'active minority'—whose importance in this crisis was clear to everyone. Don't these ideas seem to you to be rather out of date for a political society which was believed to have become modernized over the last few years?

R.A.   The most clearly visible manifestations of the revolution—or non-revolution—of May (people are now calling it 'the events', but let us go on using the old word, 'revolution') seemed to me, if I may so put it, to be archaistic. The students rediscovered the style of the Jacobin commune, or the commune of 1871, the style of the 'thought clubs' or 'intelligence clubs' of 1848, which A. de Tocqueville and Flaubert described with so much irony and scorn. The barricades were symbols, since they were not an effective means of defence against the police; except in cases where the barricades were erected spontaneously by the students, they were part of a well-known technique, that of throwing down a challenge to the forces of order. I am sure that one can see the hand of professional ringleaders in the way that the barricades were used to force the Government to make a choice between two alternatives which presented almost equal dangers to Authority. The Government had either to allow the students to remain masters of the streets, which would give the impression that it had lost the ability to govern, since the streets would be in the hands of rioters, or to set the police on to the students, in which case, at least during the first phase, bourgeois opinion would have been solidly with the rioters, with the students and against the C.R.S.[3] Standard manuals of riot technique recommend forcing Authority either into undertaking unpopular repression, or into a morally disastrous capitulation. The Government can be fairly criticized for having been caught napping by events and for having responded forty-eight hours later in a contradictory way, which combined the disadvantages of both alternative courses. It began with hesitant repression from Friday the 3rd May to Friday the 10th, and proceeded to a spectacular capitulation on Saturday the 11th.

To sum up: the barricades, seen as a challenge by student rioters to the forces of order, were not a reversion to an archaic technique, but something quite the opposite—the use of a technique which tends to oblige the Government either to lose face or to create martyrs. The French Government began by creating martyrs on the night from Friday to Saturday, and then lost face on the night from Saturday to Sunday. The use of old techniques gives an impression or archaism, but the techniques have changed their application. In the nineteenth century barricades were of some military use. Today they make a mere show of being militarily effective, but they retain or rediscover a psychological effect. So we have a movement from a material effect to a symbolic effect.

A.D.   I quite see what you mean. But this is an extraordinary demonstration of the way in which a modern government in a modern country is extremely vulnerable to the deliberate and able use of symbols.

R.A.   I agree. We have already discussed this vulnerability of modern societies. I would like to come back to a view which I believe to be valid although it puts an exaggerated emphasis on one aspect of the situation: the universities are based on the voluntary self-discipline of the students. No teaching is possible under police protection. Ten per cent of students determined on direct action can paralyse the work of any university. Ten per cent of professors who use their chairs to indoctrinate students can endanger the moral unity and the spiritual code of the university. In some respects, all genuinely modern industrial firms are similar to universities in that they must have the consent of the workers. If you consider a complex factory, even one using an older form of technology, as for example an automobile assembly line, every worker is expected to carry out his small part of the complex operation without a threat of sanctions constantly hanging over him. Of course, there are means of exerting pressure: there is the risk of dismissal, the danger of unemployment and so on. But even so, the day-to-day life of the organization depends on the co-operation of what Auguste Comte called the 'sociétaires'—the members of the whole. The founder of positivism declared that the industrial order was similar to the military order, with the difference that the industrial hierarchy did not exclude the community of sociétaires. I am afraid, however, that he was deluding himself as to the degree of participation enjoyed by workers in a modern factory. It is true that, to an ever greater degree, the boss, the manager is seen less and less as an object of hatred; instead the 'object of hatred' is coming more and more to be the system as a whole. And this is an explanation of one of the peculiar characteristics of the May revolution. In the universities there were no direct or personal attacks saying that such and such a professor was good or bad, conservative or revolutionary; the students were less against the professors than the system as a whole. Similarly, in most firms the system came in for far more denunciation than individuals. In the University there was some settling of personal scores, but between colleagues, between *assistants* or *maîtres-assistants* and professors.

So we come back to our formula. Vulnerability, certainly yes, in the sense that the element of voluntary self-discipline, the complexity of co-operation essential to the functioning of a modern society, makes it easier for minorities to take paralysing action. But on the other hand, the majority of ordinary people are well aware that their existence depends on general

76

co-operation. In a period of revolutionary excitement they dream of changing the world, but once this stage is over, they know full well that if they are to go on holiday, to get a weekly pay packet, to buy a car, or to see their children through school, it is essential that this system of production should go on functioning. The system clearly involves a techno-bureaucratic hierarchy whose style is susceptible of change, but which no revolution will ever eliminate. France, as General de Gaulle said, has once more set an example. France has gone further than any other country in the discovery of her own vulnerability. At the same time, the spectacular return of the party of order, which one self-respecting left-wing intellectual believes to be the result of fear, can also be explained in a way which is less hurtful to the self-esteem of the French: by an awareness of the conditions without which no society can function. The French revealed deep within themselves many themes for dissatisfaction, they released suppressed energies, many bottled up grievances. They got over their longing to talk, which had been repressed by their everyday silence, but after the event, they also felt another need at least as strong as their previous need for revolution, the need to come back to reality. I shall leave it to historians and sociologists to work out whether the French adventure is part of universal history or comic history.

A.D.   There is one type of Frenchman who seemed to me, as it turned out, to behave in a particularly interesting way. It is not too difficult to analyse the attitude of the small revolutionary minority—even if it is heterogeneous—nor of those who defended order. The most important category—and the one which is least clearly understandable—was made up of the people who had a number of various different attitudes, either all at the same time, or in parallel, or in succession. By this I mean that politically and economically they played the game of institutionalized opposition: they showed this when they were called to the polls, when they fought for their economic and social demands. And then ideologically, as you have just shown —and I think this is very important—in as far as they attacked models, systems and principles, both in the university field and

77

in the economic and social fields, their attitude was one of opposition pure and simple. How do you explain the existence of these various attitudes?

R.A.   I wonder if that question is properly put. I am not certain that the same people did in fact adopt these attitudes either at the same time or in succession. We should first examine whether and to what extent the French working class was predisposed in favour of a huge strike movement. Although it seems to me that the mass of the workers were unprepared for the events, our analysis should not exclude, as many commentators have tended to, the economic situation in which France found itself.

In spite of all the differences, the 1968 strikes did have some things in common with the strikes of 1936. And without over-stressing the parallels, I would like to make some observations on the economic aspects of the question. Since the inflationary crisis of 1962–63, Pompidou's Gaullist Government had pursued a policy which, although it cannot really be called deflationary, was aimed at slowing down price increases and expansion in an attempt to make the French economy competitive. The policy selected in 1962–63 was intended to act slowly and was accompanied by price controls. It prolonged the slowing down of growth up to a time when the Government wanted to introduce deep-seated changes into the country's economic structure (concentration). The crisis burst out just at the moment when we were beginning to see the first signs of a vigorous expansion. The figures show that over the last few years the growth of real incomes had slowed down, and had in fact become almost stationary over the last eighteen months. The rate of increase of nominal earnings was barely more than the rate of increase of the cost of living. As far as we can see from statistics, the middle and upper earned-income groups had a more substantial earnings rise than the lower paid workers, not to speak of wage earners at the minimum guaranteed wage level, who were in effect victims of Government policies or of firms working at very low profit levels. At the same time pockets of unemployment were forming in areas of declining industry, in the coal or iron mining areas, while concentration provoked anxiety and alarm among the middle-class workers, because one of its effects was an increase in unemployment among white collar workers made redundant as a result of the necessary modernization which it involved. In the end there was a nationwide fear of mass unemployment, unknown in France since 1945. How many unemployed were there? To give a firm and indisputable figure, we would have to agree on a definition of unemployment and on an interpretation of unemployment statistics, but no one has the slightest doubt that among young people appearing for the first time in the labour market, a substantial number (although a statistically small percentage) were unable to find work. The number of unemployed is given as somewhere between 400,000 and 500,000. Some of the young ones could not find work because they did not have the required qualifications, while others had a diploma or other paper qualification but could not be sure of finding a use for it in the commercial world. These then were the major facts of the economic situation in which the May crisis blew up: there was a restraint on wage growth, an increasing inequality between lower paid and higher paid workers, pockets of unemployment, and a fear of unemployment particularly among young people but also in some middle-class circles. This fear of unemployment was reflected in a reduction in consumption. For a year previously, planning specialists had been saying that the recovery of the French economy was being slowed down by an increase in the percentage of private savings. The attitude of the French people was changing. On the one hand this inclination to save was welcome because it could have benefited investment and modernization; these savings were, however, only being placed in short term investment, and they revealed a vague anxiety about the future rather than any renewed confidence.

The economic situation is certainly not enough to explain the violence of the convulsions of May, but there is quite reliable information which suggests that most trade unions were preparing to make claims in the autumn of 1968 and did not want to move into battle just before the summer, at a time of year

79

when the workers were already thinking about their holidays. At the same time the French Government had given the unions even less room to manoeuvre by its reluctance to meet the civil servants' wage demands. Their salaries had increased year by year, but the rate of increase was consistently lower than what they had demanded. So there was a stockpile of wage claims pending from railwaymen, postal workers and other parts of the public sector. This potential suddenly came to life when the events at Nanterre and the Sorbonne gave the impression of an earthquake, of a victory for the rioters, of Government weakness.

The strikes for wages looked as if they aimed at insurrection because of the way they happened simultaneously, and then spread and multiplied, but in this context it is as well to remember that the strikes of 1936 were not aimed at the overthrow of Léon Blum's Government. Those broke out after the election of a popular-front government. In one way the May '68 phenomenon is comparable to the '36 phenomenon but I am not forgetting the various obvious differences. There can be no question of equating the slowing down of expansion from 1963–68 with the deflation of 1931–36, although the '60's were the first time that the French economy had been exposed to the hard world of international competition and to the rigours of change in an atmosphere of decelerated expansion. The second difference is contained in the slogan 'This is not a matter of wage claims, but of dignity and participation.'

Let us say first that the Gaullist formulas for participation do not seem to arouse much interest among the trade unions, or at least among those who claim to speak for the trade unions. This point is not without importance: the union leaders do not believe that these words represent real ideas or key slogans for the mass of people by whom they were appointed.

But this does not make it any less true that the opposition to the hierarchy in the universities, in research departments, in newspaper offices, in industry, in the civil service, reveals— beyond the mere contagion or the dementia of revolution— genuine longings or ambitions, regrets or hopes, and in any case a general malaise. In attempting an interpretation of these

phenomena of which I have little direct knowledge I am reduced, of course, to relying on impressions. A sociologist, even a
scientific sociologist can describe the recent crisis better than he
can understand it.

The French system of organization and authority is a combination of a certain element of tradition with rational demands.
Sometimes the power of decision is concentrated exaggeratedly
at the summit: the specific authority of a high position of power
takes on a kind of aristocratic superiority. The style of human
relationships is still affected by the stress laid on hierarchy,
although the hierarchy, with its purely techno-bureaucratic
functions, ought not to exclude freer and more egalitarian
personal relationships.

The French have tended to introduce a techno-bureaucratic
hierarchy, which is characteristic of all modern societies, into
the framework of a society formed either by the aristocracy or
by the inequalities of bureaucratically-formulated legislation. I
have spoken about this in the context of the University. An
agrégé, teaching in a *lycée*, finds himself out-ranking once-and-
for-all a *certifié*, no matter what the respective professional
merits of each are. A graduate of the *École Polytechnique*
belongs to a privileged caste which is forever closed to the
engineer who studied at the *École des Arts et Métiers*.

Altogether French society has given a powerful place to hierarchy, a tendency for which it tries to compensate by making
constant and determined demands for equality. This permanent
contradiction seems to me to have taken on a new form during
the events of May 1968, a form which was due to the grievances,
the demands and upheaval of the salaried classes rather than
the workers. Perhaps the most unusual aspect of the May revolution was the rôle played in it by part of the bourgeoisie.

The most active elements in the University were often revolutionaries from the 16th arrondissement of Paris, or *assistants* or
maîtres-assistants, a *petite bourgeoisie* within a larger bourgeois
society, rather than the proletariat within a bourgeois society.
In industrial firms, the office and junior managerial staff often
felt themselves to be in a false position between the workers who

were demanding a wage increase and the management which did not consider them as taking part in the control of the enterprise. Now here I can see a genuine grievance with a real significance, which has nothing to do with the Student Commune, and which if I may say so is the modern element in this seemingly libertarian revolt. Participation and association are words which imply all or nothing, but the decentralization of decision-making, the circulation of information, and the giving of a feeling of responsibility to the largest possible number of people collaborating in the work of any firm are all part of the human modernization of an economy. The May events led to a confusion between anarcho-syndicalism and the self-management of a firm, between a nineteenth-century Utopia and making modern organizations more flexible, which both the rationalization and the humanization of industrial society require. Thus the revolution was anachronistic in its dream of the commune, or of 'the factory in the workers' hands' or of student power, and futuristic, despite its Utopian language, in that it opposed the sclerosis of organizational structures and authority based not on knowledge or competence but on an unconditional and unjustified sense of hierarchy. I do not know whether I am making myself clear. The events of May, like all historic movements, yoked together the best with the worst, a Utopia which could be achieved only in illusion, with useful demands expressed in confused terms. And from all this derives the contradiction which exists between various judgments of the events made by men of good faith.

A.D.   There is one theory which has been fairly widely expressed. This hypothesis suggests that those members of the salaried class—not the managers this time—who originally went beyond short-term demands and took up the cause of *contestation globale*,[4] of outright challenge to all established authority, and who then finally, (at least some of them) voted for the party of order, did so as a result of pricks of conscience. This theory also has it that for some people the outcome of the crisis was the realization that in a city like ours movements challenging authority must carefully select the form in which they express themselves.

R.A.   Yes, I think we should now consider the relationship between opposition in the University, opposition to the structure of industry and society, wage claims and finally Gaullism, which is where we started off. Gaullism seemed to be in danger, and actually was in danger for perhaps three days, from forces which had risen up from the depths of the nation. What is Gaullism's share of responsibility for the events? And what aspects of Gaullism were really under attack?

As far as the origins of the crisis are concerned, General de Gaulle's external financial policy, which aimed at maintaining a strong currency, and attempted to force a reform of the international monetary system by accumulating gold reserves, was one of the causes underlying an exaggeratedly restrictive domestic policy. The economic situation would have caused less dissatisfaction if the Government had taken the risk of a temporary deficit in the balance of payments, which would have been a minor risk in view of France's huge gold reserves. The Government's punishment fitted its crime. It wanted to undermine the soft dollar by keeping the franc hard. The franc gave way first in this strange contest, not externally but internally. The French economy could not support the excessive hardness of the franc, which had meant for the past year that French expansion relied essentially on exports and that internal consumption was lagging.

There is a second element which I think should also be criticized. Gaullism has considerably worsened the structural defects in French society. Bureaucratic centralization in France had existed before 1958, but this administrative centralization has been still further strengthened, primarily by the reduction of the rôle of Parliament to a minimum. The Members of Parliament acted as intermediaries between the electorate and their constituencies, and the administration—Authority. As such the members were probably playing a useful but little-known part.

Secondly, the Gaullist régime often selected its ministers from the ranks of the civil service, and they used a form of authority typical of civil servants, who are often remarkable men, but not politicians. By contrast M. Edgar Faure brought the style of the

Third or Fourth Republic back into relations with the farmers. He was much criticized for making what were called demagogic concessions, and for slowing down the modernization of agriculture. Maybe the concessions he made were rationally untenable, but every government in a democratic country has to try to find a way of reconciling what a rational policy requires with the demands of individual groups who would suffer from the application of policy. General de Gaulle's ministers reigned like very senior civil servants, steeped in the authoritarian tradition, and insufficiently skilled in true political dialogue. The politician listens to his electors, but also to his officials who tell him what the rational policy should be: he then proceeds to produce a compromise, which can never be perfect, between the demands of the electors and the advice of the officials.

Centralization in France has been emphasized by the authoritarian and bureaucratic style adopted by many of those who served in the Government. Most people who work directly for the State in France, Members of Parliament or officials, give the impression that within themselves they have, or at all events believe that they have, something of the magnificence of Louis XIV. When the sovereign himself is a kind of Sun King, little monarchs are established in descending order well down into the hierarchy. I have the impression that many Frenchmen eventually found this rather irritating! No one likes to be treated as an inferior merely because he serves his country without submitting himself wholly and unconditionally to the will of the Prince.

General de Gaulle has never concealed his passionate love for France, but he never showed the French people the same consideration which he showed for the idea of France. It may well be that the feeling that the Government was rather scornful of the governed was responsible in part for the satisfaction that some Frenchmen felt during May when the Gaullist régime was in difficulty. Although they may subsequently have voted for the Gaullists again, that merely proved that they preferred a Gaullist Government to a vacuum, but not that they had reconciled themselves at all deeply to it and its manner of government.

If the essential thing in the politics of Gaullist France was that

84

no crisis could be resolved except at the highest level, it may be said that the Gaullist régime pushed the vulnerability of the entire Government to any accidental attack to an absurd point. We have discussed this in the context of the University—Cohn-Bendit's revolt led to the closure of Nanterre and the Sorbonne, to a challenge to the authority of M. Peyrefitte, to a consideration of the matter by the Cabinet, and finally to the intervention of the President of the Republic himself. General de Gaulle claimed that a popular mandate invested him with supreme authority of law. He interpreted his Constitution in such a way that his Prime Minister was the expression of his own policies, and as a result he could not be seen as an arbiter between the parties but occupied the position of a real Chief Executive. The authority of the Prime Minister could not be questioned without questioning that of the President of the Republic, and a non-Gaullist Chamber could not be elected without creating a crisis for the régime. So General de Gaulle achieved the result he wanted: he condemned France to be 100 per cent Gaullist or to fall apart. The May crisis arose in a régime which rested so much on the magic of one man that if the charisma of the Head of State were affected, the State and society would collapse along with him. In the June elections, the French people were condemned by General de Gaulle to show themselves 100 per cent Gaullists, because they had realized in May that the other alternative was an absolute void. So the Gaullist régime was itself responsible both for its death and its resurrection, for its collapse and its triumph. The danger which the régime has for the nation was clearly revealed in May, but precisely because the danger took the form of a catastrophe, the majority preferred to choose the alternative.

One final point. The general challenge to authority stems in part from national psychology, and is the result of the continuing hierarchical authoritarian repression which stretches far back in time, and although it is taking new forms in modern society, it has not disappeared.

A.D.   This leads us directly to the problem of the tactics used by the various parties which were active during the crisis, whose motivation you have just analysed, and to what you think of these tactics.

R.A.   I have met intelligent, reasonable men who are convinced that there was a kind of invisible bandmaster. Some people think he was Chinese, others American—the inevitable C.I.A.—and some who even think he was Chinese and American simultaneously! Commentators of this kind find it very hard to resist the temptation to discern reason lying behind irrationality, to see a human will overcoming chaos. They would like an event which the historian can comprehend in a single glance, to have had a single actor. They refuse to allow the possibility that the events might have come as a surprise, might have deceived or overcome the actors. No-one is able yet to have any really fixed and certain views on this, and so I shall only give you some of my impressions.

There were revolutionary action groups in the universities, in the factories, and in the *lycées*. The most effective of them were set up in advance, for example the *Lycée Action Groups*—the *C.A.L.*[5] organized by a section of the P.S.U. party secretariat. In the *lycées* the revolt was not spontaneous, but came to the fore as a result of the favourable climate—through the action of an organization set up in advance. It is possible, although there is no proof, that the group of *enragés* of Nanterre was part of an international organization, the Students for a Democratic Society, the S.D.S. in America and the S.D.S. in Germany. Maybe these groups are united via some clandestine organization, or perhaps they merely use similar methods to express the malaise of students in all countries, or maybe the similarities are symptoms of a contagion. I think it is probable that the revolutionary groups may have received financial help from various sources, but again I have no proof of this. I do not think that very considerable funds would have been needed to promote the events of May and June. In general I have little faith in the detective-story interpretation of history, and in particular I don't believe in the conspiracy interpretation of the May disturbances. But of course I cannot prove that the C.I.A. took no part in it—how can you prove a negative? I cannot prove that there was no Chinese headquarters somewhere, although no one seems to know of one. There is no difficulty in reconstructing the mechanism of the events without supposing the existence of a manipulator. If indeed such a person existed, then he was very intelligent, but he was not indispensable. The development of the crisis is intelligible enough through the actions and reactions of the various participants.

The revolutionary groups acted with ingenuity and intelligence, and in the first phase were helped by the clumsy reactions of the Government (which was certainly not manipulated either by the C.I.A. or the Chinese) on the one hand and by the solidarity of the Parisian middle class with the students (and this too cannot be put down to the wiles of the Americans or the Chinese) on the other. If we consider the way in which the idea of occupying the universities spread, it becomes immediately apparent that this is what the groups wanted, and there was no need for an overall organizer: it was enough for every university to have small groups of students affiliated to the P.S.U. or to the two Trotskyite groups (the J.C.R. and the F.E.R.).[6] In the situation which arose after 14th May these little groups were in charge. Why bother to dream up what the English call a 'master-mind'? It is true that the situation can be validly analysed as a vicious circle in which agitation led to repression which in turn resulted in increasing agitation. The machinery operated, but there was no need for a politbureau of superior intelligence to conceive and organize the process in advance.

Let us leave on one side the revolutionary groups who accomplished the rôle which they had taken on, and who acted as they were bound to act as a result of their views. The leading actors were the Communist Party and the C.G.T., the Federation (of socialist parties) and the Government.

Everyone knew that the Communist Party did not want to overthrow the Government by insurrection. On the other hand it played a part in aggravating the crisis by issuing strike orders, in particular the orders it gave for unlimited strikes in sectors where it had overwhelming influence. Why did it give these orders? The current explanation has it that it did so for fear of

87

being overtaken by left-wing groups. In other words the Communist Party unleashed strikes and the occupation of factories because it was afraid of leaving the monópoly of revolutionary action in the hands of Trotskyites, young workers, revolutionary Marxist-Leninists, pro-Chinese groups or Castroites, and thus loosing its control over the masses. Let us accept this explanation. I wonder, however, whether the Communist Party did not make a mistake. I wonder whether, in its attempt to maintain its control over the working masses by drowning the original movement to occupy factories in a much more general movement which it directed, the Party did not end up as the sorcerer's apprentice. In the end it pushed the crisis to the point at which, on Monday 27th May, it launched the 'popular government' slogan, and created the impression that it was working for the overthrow of the Gaullist government by semi-insurrectional methods. The paradox is that it wanted nothing of the kind, because the policy it had decided on, which we have already discussed, was to come back into French political life in the hope of reaching a coalition with the rest of the left. To avoid being overtaken on the left it played a part in the progressive broadening of strikes and occupation of the factories, for which in retrospect it appeared to most people to have been responsible. Also with the aim of avoiding being overtaken, it often accepted a show of hands vote in factories, and did not insist on a secret ballot. It did not want to overthrow the Gaullist government, which in its turn constantly relied on the Party to avoid a real revolution; the Communists, however, played such a part in the general uproar that one would need to be very subtle or very detached to clear them of all responsibility for events, which seemed almost insurrectional.

I would like to take up the same idea in a different way: no one believed any more in the idea of a general strike; it was thought of as a myth derived from the early twentieth-century Sorelians.[7] The Communist Party managed, without wanting to, to accomplish the remarkable feat of reviving the myth of the general strike to a certain degree (although in fact there was no general strike properly so-called, not even in Paris, far less in

France as a whole) but the Party explained afterwards that it had no evil intentions. Everyone who demanded a general strike saw it as a revolutionary way of taking power. The argument that a pseudo-general strike could be called with the aim of securing a 10 per cent wage increase could hardly be taken seriously by anyone. Thus the Communist Party, which for the time being is conservative, behaved in a way which forced the average Frenchman to conclude that it was motivated either by great malice or great stupidity. Let us say that the Communist Party was the victim of the P.S.U., the troublemakers and the *groupuscules*, and hence of the intellectuals—which could be said to be a fair return for some of the things that have happened in the past.

A.D.   Do you think it could have used different tactics at this time?

R.A.   I don't know. To answer this question one would have had to have been in most parts of France, and to have visited the factories. I cannot make any exact assessments of the degree to which the Party has been weakened in large factories and undertakings, and nor can I judge the depths of revolutionary feeling in part of the working class, which the Party did not want to lose. I am tempted in retrospect to say that it might have been to the advantage of the Communist Party to have chosen different tactics (although I am no longer sure of this today). It has not won back the revolutionary groups, it has lost a proportion of its passive supporters, and within the next few months or years at least, it is going to be obliged either to set off new disturbances or to start again from scratch the operation it has been building up over the last ten years.

The Communist Party suffers from the contradiction which plagued Europe's social democrats from the end of the nineteenth century to 1940. It is not possible to go on talking indefinitely as a revolutionary, making stern condemnations of Gaullist government and personal power, while giving so many observers, even not specially clear-sighted ones, the feeling that you want anything except a violent revolution.

This contradiction becomes particularly striking if we compare

the words and the actions of the Party. The French Communist Party is prey to another contradiction as well. Externally
it conducts itself in a partly social-democratic way, while within
itself it retains a semi-Stalinist structure. It has changed neither
its organization nor its way of thinking. As an outside observer,
I would like to see the Communist Party become a social-
democratic party, for France can have no stabilized modern
régime until the Communist Party has become a socialist party
which agrees to represent working-class interests and press for
reforms, without maintaining close links with the Soviet Union
and without striving to introduce into France a form of industrial society which the nation as a whole rejects. This process has
been indefinitely interrupted as a result of the events of May
1968. The only people who are pleased about this are those who
want a violent revolution, who believe a violent revolution to be
possible, and who imagine that were it to happen, it would not
end in Leninism or in Stalinism. Those who are pleased about
the interruption of the process are in my view either nihilists
who want to destroy without knowing what to build in place of
what they destroy, or Utopians who imagine that the régime
which would arise after a violent revolution could be something
other than despotic. But I admit that the Utopia of *auto-gestion*
(self-management) has found favour with the intellectuals.

The Federation (of socialist parties) only played a real, effective part for a few days. At the beginnings of May, it thought no
harm, and did not foresee the explosion any more than you or I.
The moderate left, and particularly M. Mendès-France, for
whom I have great personal respect, immediately came down
on the side of the students. They were in opposition, and they
saw the students as a symbol of a revolt of youth against the
France of grand-papa. It would probably be wrong to criticize
them for the support they gave to the student revolt against
authority—it was a reflex action. They played no part, or
hardly any part in the strike movements. The Force-Ouvrière[8]
unions and the C.F.D.T. overbid the C.G.T.,[9] particularly the
C.F.D.T.[10] which was more concerned in reforms in the structure of industrial undertakings than in large claims. But the

C.F.D.T. and the F.O. unions are not connected with the Federation.[11] At one point M. Descamp[12] proposed M. Mendès-France as Prime Minister in a caretaker cabinet, but M. Mendès-France had not suggested this to Descamp. The Federation had no responsibility for the strike movement: but it found something to be pleased about in the movement, because every opposition in France finds pleasure in any difficulties experienced by the Government, according to the unwritten law of *dirty business*, of politics considered not as an art but as a kind of sport in which any means, or almost any, are legitimate.

There remains the rôle of the Federation—a rôle from which the ruin of the Federation derives—in the period from 24th to 30th May, and particularly from the 28th to the 30th. The Federation feared the overthrow of the Gaullist government by revolt, for its leaders knew that in a revolutionary period the Federation, despite the fact that it had more members in Parliament, would be weaker than the Communist Party. M. Guy Mollet and M. Mitterrand were perfectly well aware of the fact that a government under the title of a Left Union, which was possible in a calm period, would run the risk in a revolutionary period of sliding towards a 'people's democracy'. Neither M. Mitterrand nor M. Guy Mollet had the slightest desire to suffer a coup like that of 1948 in Prague. Neither of them had enough confidence in the Communist Party lightheartedly to accept the risk of an adventure of this kind. Between 28th and 30th May the leaders of the Federation were either the victims of collective madness or tricked by General de Gaulle. For three days the most percipient observers wondered whether a régime founded by one man, and based on him alone, was going to collapse with him. The unfortunate speech of 24th May gave further currency to the feeling that authority was crumbling. The crisis affected social discipline: it seemed that no one was obeying orders any more in business, in industry and in research departments. Transport and communications services were on strike, and the civil services of ministries were having their own revolutions. Sometimes departmental heads were paying court to their new masters and turned their backs on their former bosses. Three days of great fear or of great illusion, which made fools of many. People with good heads on their shoulders thought they were witnesses not of the end of a civilization, but of the end of a man and of a régime.

The Federation's members shared the madness of Paris, and they poured out intemperate declarations via non-government radio stations. M. Mitterrand proposed himself as President of the Republic and he offered M. Mendès-France the job of heading a caretaker government. These proposals seemed to pay no heed to the text of the Constitution. If the President of the Republic had retired, M. Monnerville[13] would automatically have become the interim President, and the Prime Minister would have stayed in office. It is true that this kind of argument coming from the Gaullists was not entirely free of hypocrisy; General de Gaulle too, had sometimes forgotten the Constitution. Moreover the régime was so closely bound up with the person of the President of the Republic, who had bound up his fate so closely with that of his Prime Minister that it was not difficult to imagine what would happen when General de Gaulle retired to his village and his sorrows. Even M. Giscard d'Estaing proposed that M. Pompidou should resign. The fact is, however, that the Federation, which wanted to pay General de Gaulle back in his own coin, that is to do in 1968 what General de Gaulle had done in 1958, and take advantage of a quasi-revolt to provoke the fall of a government while at the same time giving a cover of legality to the succeeding government, was hoist with its own petard, or caught by General de Gaulle's wiles. When the General said 'I am not going', M. Mitterrand's candidature for the office of the President of the Republic, which was not vacant, and M. Mendès-France's offer to form a caretaker government for the transitional period, when there was no transition, looked in retrospect like participation in an attempt to undermine the State. A strange performance, almost a comic performance in the last analysis, but with innumerable actors. Several Gaullist deputies begged the Prime Minister to persuade the General to retire, etc. A very large part of Paris politics shared this mental derangement.

So the Federation made its fatal mistake. On the one hand it made common cause with a movement which while not genuinely revolutionary had every appearance of being so, and on the other, it put forward proposals incompatible with the text of the Constitution.

Certainly, I say again, the respect that General de Gaulle has shown for his own Constitution has been intermittent enough for the observer to find excuses for the mistakes of the opposition. But unfortunately politics has a cast-iron rule—you must succeed. There can be no pardon for violations of the Constitution by those who fail. Nations do not like the defeated.

So let us go on to the winners. The winners were losers too, for in this affair which no one can really be said to have won, there was one genuine loser: the whole of France. Those intellectuals who unleash their sarcasm on me—and to whom I do the same in return—celebrate the days of May as the dawn of liberty or of revolution. The editorial of *Temps Modernes* declares that one thing has been proved, that a revolution can succeed without, or against the Communist Party. I do not exclude the possibility that the revolutionaries may create further disturbances, serious disturbances, in France. In all probability they will fail. And even if they succeed in part, they will accumulate debris. They will not succeed in imposing what they call a socialist régime on a country which is three parts hostile. Even those who claim to be in favour of it do not understand the nature of such a régime and would hate its institutions.

It seems to me that Gaullism, despite its electoral victory, is weakened. Whether General de Gaulle and his government bear a greater or a lesser share of responsibility for the explosion is a subject for endless inconclusive discussion by historians. I do not feel able to give any answer. But the régime and its leader, the only man able to resolve the crisis, came out winners! The Federation was overwhelmed, the Communist Party is disoriented, and except in the universities, the small revolutionary groups remain much as they were, perhaps somewhat less dangerous because they have been unmasked. André Malraux seems, in appearance at least, to have been right when he said

'There are we, the Communists, and nothing else.' There are a few points to consider, even so. In the first ballot the Gaullists still fail to secure an absolute majority of votes. If a system of proportional ballotting were to be introduced tomorrow, you would find that what Maurice Duverger[14] has called 'le marais', the part of the French people which stretches from the Socialist Party to half-way across the right, represents distinctly more than half the electorate. The combination of the Gaullists, the Communists and nothing more is a result of the system of voting for one candidate only in two rounds of voting. As France is governed on the basis of a lawfully determined electoral system, and as the rules of electoral competition decide the party structure, Gaullism, within the established system, has achieved one of its objectives, that of making it for the moment impossible for France to have any government other than one which derives from General de Gaulle and the Gaullist Constitution. It leaves opponents of Gaullism with no methods other than ineffective proposals and ill-considered actions. Whether this result is worthy of admiration or not, it has been achieved.

Although M. Pompidou may have made some erroneous decisions, his prestige gained considerably. He and only he was continuously in evidence from his return from Asia to the end of the crisis. All the information media were turned on him, and he appeared as a man who was supporting the State by himself. He was a statesman by virtue of two qualities which are often little recognized but which are pre-eminent—physical endurance and complete control of his nerves. He was able to go without sleep for three consecutive nights, to show up well on television after sleepless nights, to negotiate with trade union representatives for ten, twelve or fifteen hours at a time. This is a kind of performance well beyond most people's powers, and not what you expect of a man who has come to politics after being a teacher. In a crisis period this quiet strength is of incomparable value. M. Pompidou seems never to have lost his head, and he always retained his confidence in his implicit agreement with the Communist Party. Could he have done better or worse in the Grenelle negotiations? Should he have stopped General de Gaulle going to Rumania? Was he right in opening a parliamentary debate before General de Gaulle had spoken? Did he make excessive concessions in the Grenelle agreements? Specialists may debate these questions, but for the public at large, mistakes do not count.

His position as dauphin, as heir-apparent, seemed to have been strengthened. Has he been a victim of his very success, a success at which the Prince might take umbrage? Have the secret talks between the two men in May left a bitter taste? Is M. Pompidou willing to leave it to others to apply M. Capitant's ideas on participation? I am not going to attempt to sort out these hypotheses which could all contain part of the truth. At all events, if General de Gaulle wished to rule within the administration in the same way as he reigned in public, he had to rid himself of a Prime Minister who had acquired an authority of his own.

Gaullist power, including General de Gaulle himself, has been attacked by a substantial part of the country. For a régime which for ten years has governed France with more authority than any other French Government has ever possessed, the discovery that there was such a fund of violence and indignation in the masses must have been both staggering and bitter. Foreigners saw France revealed as being weaker than they had believed, and the French people more divided than they had imagined. The façade of stability and magnificence has so to speak collapsed, and foreign observers have discovered what my macabre humour calls eternal France: *Omnia Gallia divisa est*—All Gaul is divided. Gaullist fiction has it that General de Gaulle had brought the French people together. The least that can be said is that the proof of this bringing together has still to be seen.

A.D. Finally, there is one point which it is difficult to avoid raising at this time. Gaullism seems to be a camp within France and yet at the same time it wants to represent the whole of France.

R.A. The point you have raised is one that I have been racking my brains over for a long time, ever since I started thinking about French politics. It is a question to which I always have great difficulty in giving a definite answer.

95

When one ponders the division of France into two camps, there is one answer which springs spontaneously to mind. If one has a system of majority voting, then inevitably two camps are formed either at the first or second round of voting. No one talks of England being divided into two camps for the simple reason that the Labour Party and the Conservative Party alternate in office. The two camps in France have a significance quite different from the two parties in Britain for the simple reason that the Communist Party is not yet integratèd into the normal pattern of French politics. Most Frenchmen would see a government dominated by the Communist Party as essentially different from the Labour government. On the other hand I do not subscribe to the exaggeratedly pessimistic interpretation which says that those Frenchmen who vote for the Federation, the Communist Party or the P.S.U., about 40–45 per cent of the electorate, are in a state of internal exile. Those Frenchmen who do not vote for the Gaullists in the first ballot, that is more than half the electorate, do not see themselves as being for this reason placed outside the city wall, not represented in the State. The French tragedy since 1789 has been summed up in a most striking formula by Emmanuel Berl: 'France is always governed by a gang.' Let us restate that in chaste language—Renan's language: since 1789 part of the French elite has always considered itself to be in a state of internal exile. France has yet to find a régime in which the political battle is conducted according to firm rules, which are acceptable even to those who are out of office, because they have the ambition and opportunity to succeed to power themselves by legal means. Is the régime as a whole, with its laws and methods of operation recognized as legitimate by the population at large? One of the annoying consequences of the May crisis is that the possibility of the overthrow of the legal government by revolt has once again emerged as a possibility. It has once again appeared on the political horizon.

Gaullism had a dramatic success by means of the electoral law after a period of acute crisis, but it still has enemies: on the one hand, there is part of the working class which, whether it is revolutionary or not, may yet again feel alienated and frustrated because of the disproportion between the dream and the reality, between the claims which were made and the advantages which were actually gained. On the other hand, Gaullism has been rejected still more radically by part of the intelligentsia, of the intellectual class. This is not merely a rejection of the present Government, but of any government which might be able to operate in a society like ours.

According to some of the first interpretations of the May revolution, the enemy power which the revolts, the barricades and the passionate speeches were supposed to overthrow once and for all, can be defined in the first place by the lack of contact between those who led and those who carried out orders. The law which the *enragés* challenged was the iron law of the oligarchy, to use a phrase from current sociological literature. The general assemblies in the faculties, with teachers and students of all categories and all degrees of competence taking part, the way in which delegates once elected could be so easily recalled, the apparent freedom of open-ended random discussion together with directed movements of the masses, all these practices were a symbolic rejection of the apparatus, of general staffs and of bureaucracy.

Now the events have convinced some intellectuals that a revolution of this kind, in defiance of the Communist Party, against the pessimists who keep the industrial society dedicated to the hierarchic order, is now a real possibility. They say that if the Communist Party had wished it, the workers' revolt, taking over from the student revolt, would have led to the fall of the régime. The revolution which the heirs of the Stalinists said was impossible because they feared it, the revolution which the sociologists regarded as out of the question through conservatism, on the pretext that modern societies necessarily entail authoritarian and rational control, that revolution almost happened. It was within a hand's reach. It was prevented by the Communists far more than repulsed by the Government.

Could the political régime have been swept away in the tempest? Perhaps, although the answer to this question must remain forever inconclusive. But even if we accept that the revolutionaries were right, and that a French government is still at the mercy of street movements as it was in the nineteenth century, the lesson to be drawn from the events is far from that which the 'libertarians' draw from it. The Hungarian revolution of 1956 won its victory over authority and the victors were preparing to 'restore' a pluralist parliamentary democracy. What kind of government would have been set up in France by the victors ranging from Cohn-Bendit to Mendès-France and Waldeck-Rochet?

The historian has a choice between two hypotheses. A Mendès-France government? France would have come back to the situation of 1936 or 1944 with an incomparably weaker moderate left. A Mendès-France–Waldeck-Rochet government? France would have followed the road which Czechoslovakia took soon after its liberation. Neither the Student Commune nor MM. Geismar and Sauvageot would have been of any consequence as soon as tearing up paving stones gave place to the administration of affairs and the government of people.

The events did not provide the slightest beginnings of proof of the revolutionaries' case, nor even any argument in favour of it. The revolutionaries believe themselves to be post-Marxists, and derive their theories from well before Marx. No economic, political or social order which differed both from the Soviet and the Western model saw the light of day. The days of May are really remarkable for one thing—and I do not underestimate its importance—which was the apparent rejection of modern society at a time of a general crisis of authority and obedience (as was maintained). The provinces lagged behind Paris, and the fact that workers were not working did not make them into willing strikers. The nine million strikers are indeed as much a part of the legend of the glorious weeks as were the famous 75,000 who were shot.[15] In short, if the Revolution was averted only by the refusal of the Communist Party to be involved, the sociologists will have to admit that a relatively liberal régime can suffer the same fate as a totalitarian régime like that in Stalinist Hungary. The sociologist will return to the view of the classical philosophers that political régimes may be corrupted without this corruption being the result of an outdated system of production, and without it necessarily leading to a modification of such a system or of property law. There is not the slightest reason to subscribe to the new madness of the Paris intellectuals, the madness of dreaming of a libertarian revolution in the industrial age, of self-management as a constituent principle of a society which would at last be free, neither capitalist nor soviet.

One writer whom the gods have not over-favoured with their gifts, has put the essential point without, however, giving an answer: 'Seen from a rational, economic point of view, such demands are perhaps Utopian.' And he adds wisely 'which I will neither confirm nor deny'. But at the same time he restricts himself to pointing out 'a state of mind which must be taken into account' (I agree) and he leaves the significance of the event in suspense. In 1792, 1848 and 1871, the people of Paris wholly succumbed to the dream of the commune. With equal regularity the French people, terrified by their own actions, have rebuilt a bureaucratic hierarchy from the ruins of the old hierarchy. I hope that on this occasion they will make better use of a pseudo-revolution (since the Student Commune lived under the former government, which now has the job of liquidating the revolution). But the Communes—the most spectacular was the Sorbonne Commune, with others in the faculties, in research departments and in the C.N.R.S.—did not direct anything at all, they proposed a number of reforms some of which dealt with salary scales, and others with the division of power, some imbued with corporative spirit, others with anarcho-syndicalist utopianism.

If we believe the prophets of the revolution, imagination was in power. When I read the proposals developed by most of the communes or the commissions, I am forced to conclude that imagination was not very imaginative.

4

Gaullists and Intellectuals

A.D.   Many people have said that this was a revolution without aims or ideology. It has also been said that our entire society
was being challenged. I would like to know your point of view
about that.

R.A.   It seems to me that both these statements are true,
and that they are complementary, not contradictory. The only
ideology of the student revolt which was started by the March
22nd Movement, was the rejection of every kind of discipline.
The students claimed to belong to the anarchist tradition, which
may be an ideology, but one which is profoundly incompatible
with the organization of a modern society. The organization—
if you can call it that—of the Student Commune had something
of the manner of direct democracy with some libertarian aspects.
There was something appealing about its anarchic disorder.
Very few people were prevented from speaking, even those who
were opposed to the ideas of the majority. There was plenty of
uproar and confusion at meetings, but the uproar was almost
always good-humoured. The very existence of the crowd and
the mood of these meetings exerted pressure on the teaching
staff, but there was hardly ever anything that could be described
as physical violence. Indeed, people who were far more closely
concerned in the events than I was have told me that the student

revolt very rarely came to personal attack on individual professors. The teachers settled old scores between themselves, but
the students did not, at least not in the Sorbonne. (Things were
different in the Faculty of Medicine.) They did not show themselves to be better disposed to liberal professors than to authoritarian ones; the revolt was directed against the university
system with its traditional order and its apparently imposed discipline. There were one or two instances which suggest that the
students wanted to desecrate some places which were loaded
with social prestige. I am afraid that I cannot reproduce the
exact words of an inscription which the Nanterre students wrote
on a staff-room wall, but the gist of it was 'We have made love
in your sanctuary.' This is a revealing story in a way—the staff
hardly think of their staff-room as a holy place. It looks as if the
students took a particular pleasure in breaking taboos and cast-
ing down idols.

Some commentators became enthusiastic for direct democracy, and radio listeners one day heard a Gaullist—he is a
minister now—singing a duet with a well-known journalist in
praise of the incomparable merits of direct democracy. This was
a strange illusion to be accepted by men who before all this were
responsible, serious-minded people, and who are responsible,
serious-minded people again today. We know what direct democracy with no permanent delegation of authority, no constituent assembly, means. It is a dream inversion—experienced
during insurrectional crises—of society as it really is, where
administrators are permanent, where bureaucrats have authority, and where power is not exercised by what Sartre calls the
'*groupe en fusion*'. Even Athenian democracy, which at its height
included only about 40,000 citizens, did not practise total direct
democracy. It is quite inconceivable that the Faculty of Letters
in Paris, with some tens of thousands of students, or a firm like
Renault, with some tens of thousands of workers could be run on
the principle of self-management or direct democracy.

This movement, a revolt against organized authority, with
no aims other than the overthrow of this authority, produced
some insurrectional pseudo-institutions which under certain

conditions might survive the events in some form or other. By these I mean for instance the Student Commune, the plenary Assemblies or the general Assemblies. Outside the University, however, no new institutions were created which could outlive the exceptional circumstances which gave them birth. Disturbances similar to those in the universities spread through all strata of society. Why did research institutions strike? Why did the industrial research departments of some big firms not merely strike but continue their strike after the crisis was over? So we have to admit that the revolt against authority—any authority—had its echoes in society at large, which implies that there was a predisposition to revolution in that society, and this in turn reveals the extent to which society itself was challenged. It also shows a deep dissatisfaction with the state of affairs, or at least enough grievances, resentments or disillusionment to create a potential of emotion which, given the right conditions, could burst out and shatter the whole structure. Now from this I draw a conclusion which comes back to my first reply to your question. I will say first what many observers in the past said at the beginning of every nineteenth-century revolution: this was a revolution with no aim, no ideology and no plan. Proudhon, a socialist, was just as shocked and dismayed by the explosion in February 1848 as was Tocqueville who was taken for a reactionary although in fact he was a liberal. So, all right, this was a revolution with no ideology; but it was at the same time probably the most fundamental and most interesting revolution of this century, since some people see the absence of any plan as a proof that its aims were more far reaching and that it was the result of a much profounder dissatisfaction with society than any other revolution. Let us consider these two aspects. I shall start, if I may, with the second subject—this profound dissatisfaction.

I have already told you that I attach no great importance to what the main characters in a revolutionary period say. Language is far less important than people's emotional state. Language is better at expressing regrets and dreams than considered thought. But a consideration of ideological themes scrawled on walls or printed in newspapers can be of some help to us in understanding the ills of an industrial society or the criticisms levelled against it.

The first of these themes which was particularly important in the university world was the theme of democratization, or criticism of the bourgeois university, or of the conservative rôle of the University, or of bourgeois culture. I have already mentioned this subject.

It seems to me that modern society claims to be based on two historical ideas. Both are valid, yet in a certain sense they are incompatible. On the one hand we have the egalitarian, democratic idea, and on the other the idea of systematization and productivity. Within the University, direct experience and sociological analysis show that competition, which is an inevitable manifestation of the democratic idea, gives an advantage to the children of the privileged classes. We can express the same idea in a different way: modern societies use the ideology of meritocracy to reconcile the existence of actual inequality with equality of opportunity. The students challenged precisely this kind of reconciliation. To do so, they drew on the ideas which in France are attributed to Pierre Bourdieu because of his special skill in formulating them. Competition, which in theory is egalitarian, tends in practice to preserve social inequality. This was one of the major themes of criticism, and it represents a new phase in the dialectics of modern society. The first step was the idea of equality, and this led next to the suppression of legal inequalities of class or condition. Come what may, equality before the law is now an integral part of modern institutions. But in the next phase it was realized that equality established by law did not eliminate social and economic inequality which are now the target for socialist criticism. Even in the field of education, legal equality tends up to a point to perpetuate economic and social inequality. In other words, we cannot prevent the perpetuation of social inequalities handed down by the social status of the family merely by putting an end to the inheritance of wealth.

This is by no means a criticism to be despised. It could lead to some programme of action aimed at reducing inequality in education. Yet it could also move towards demagogy pure and simple, to the false idea that these conservative processes are evil in themselves, or to the illusion that there is any kind of society which could eliminate them.

Second theme: it appeared from what happened that many Frenchmen had suddenly discovered that economic progress had not been enough to end poverty, nor even less to remove considerable differences in income. The gap between a worker on the minimum guaranteed wage (S.M.I.G.—*salaire minimum interprofessionel garanti*) and a millionaire is too great to be measured with any accuracy. No one has ever claimed that economic progress alone is enough to eliminate the inequality and stratification which are typical of a modern society. What has been said—and this is still true—is that 70–80 per cent of the population benefit, although in varying degrees, from the increase in production which is made possible by economic growth. It is true enough that the fruits of this progress are distributed unjustly, if by unjustly we mean unequally. In the years immediately leading up to this explosion, this injustice could be measured precisely in the sense that the wages of the upper levels of the hierarchy rose more than those of the lower levels. This phenomenon is not typical of all industrial societies, nor indeed of all phases of the French expansion, but in this case it did happen. I mentioned the figure of 70–80 per cent. So we are left with between 20 and 30 per cent whom today we call the poor —the French poor or the American poor. These are the people whom progress has left behind, engineers of 40 who have lost their jobs because of technical developments, older people whose savings have been hit by inflation, young people who have acquired no qualifications or whose qualifications are unsuitable for the only jobs they can find, families who live in declining areas where the traditional industry is in a state of decay. And so on. A society which seeks to make rapid progress must be prepared to submit to the disciplines of modernization, of concentration and conversion of effort. The economists recognize the need for this, but many people suffer as a result. I have never held the view that our societies during the course of their development over the last twenty years, have ever approached either a state of genuine affluence or a social order which 'perfectionists' could accept as equitable. But all societies we know of, of whatever kind they may be, settle down—if we except periods of 'romantic illusion'—into a stratified, hierarchical form which no kind of society we have yet seen has ever been able to avoid. The stratification and the hierarchy of the so-called socialist societies are rather different in some respects. They probably achieve some attenuation of economic inequality, but this is offset by an accentuation of social difference, and an added weight of politico-ideological pressure. The majority of the French people are not prepared to pay such a price for a reduction in economic inequality. Moreover experience suggests that East European countries are more eager to learn economic lessons from the West than vice versa.

Now we come to the third topic, which is much farther reaching and which is in contradiction to the one we have just discussed—criticism of the consumer society. Let me begin by making a remark in bad taste, but one which is commonplace and has to be made. There is one kind of criticism of the consumer society which I find quite intolerable. This is the kind of criticism voiced by film directors at the wheels of their Ferraris, or by the rich children of the P.D.G. driving the 2CV's or 4CV's which their parents have bought them. If people genuinely find that their privileges and material possessions are a real embarrassment, there are many ways open to them of giving them up. I know some young people who loathe the consumer society who have turned their ideas into action by setting off to what we call the underdeveloped countries to find spiritual nourishment, or, if you prefer, to nurture their need for idealism. But it is something of a paradox to denounce the consumer society while at the same time helping the underdeveloped countries to progress to the point where they too will be aware of the evils of this detestable state of affairs. Whatever precise and exact meaning we attach to social and economic development, its targets are always to modernize agricultural production and industrial efficiency, and to make education readily available, in other words to arrive at all the characteristics of the modern so-called consumer society. Of course these young people—and others not so young!—would reply that they do not oppose technical progress, as Herbert Marcuse is constantly saying. They want to see a society in which affluence does not entail an obsession with success, where an increase in production is not the be-all and end-all, and in which people do not attach enormous importance to possessions. They would like to see an efficient society in which the 'quality of life' would be guaranteed. Here we come to powerful and confused ideas which it is almost impossible to discuss in rational terms.

The majority of the French population today does not despise the consumer society, if by 'consumer society' we understand a society which enables us to achieve an improvement in living standards. Instead of 'consumer society' we could just as well say 'producer society', by which I mean a society which is efficient enough in its use of agricultural and industrial labour to allow an increasing number of families to acquire what the students of the *Institut d'études politiques* and most students of the Faculty of Letters in Paris already have—in other words a steady job, enough domestic appliances to take the drudgery out of housework, and an income large enough for them to be able to give their children the chance of higher education. The rejection of the consumer society is not a definition of an aim, but the expression of an emotional and moral revolt which cannot be translated into a political programme.

Herbert Marcuse, who is taken to be one of the founders of the movement, detests modern society whether it be capitalist or socialist. A close study of his books, including a footnote in his latest book *The One Dimensional Man* reveals indeed that he hates Soviet society more than Western society, although the rest of the book is taken up with criticism of Western society. Marcuse has never offered the 'great refusal' as a political programme. He even claims that the proletariat is too well integrated into the system of production to have retained any revolutionary potential. Moreover he does not want to deprive mankind of the benefits of affluence. His dream is of a non-repressive society (in the Freudian sense) and he seems to believe in the merits of a radical

rejection of the existing order. He hopes through student violence, and in the United States through negro violence, to build
a new society which would retain the benefits of the industrial
society without exacting the price we have to pay for them
today. We are on good terms despite our disagreements, and the
last time I met him I said: 'Essentially your philosophy is to
arrive at a completely pacified society through the use of violence.' He replied 'That's exactly it.' That answer is enough on
which to judge his 'philosophy.' There has never been a case of
violence resulting in pacification, (which anyway I believe to be
incompatible with human nature). Of course, like everybody
else I subscribe to a great many of Marcuse's points of criticism.
Who could fail to denounce the nuclear arms race as madness?
But the division of mankind into sovereign states and rival ideologies is not a new thing. The nuclear arms race, which incidentally has slowed down, is just another manifestation of the
competition between sovereign states which has been going on
for millennia. No one has the slightest doubt that it is more
important for the United States to step up the fight against
poverty or to expend more resources on improving the quality
of life or on strengthening law and order in the cities than it is
to make the middle classes still better off. In the abstract no-one
would reject such manifestly reasonable ideas. But men and
societies refuse to let themselves be treated as things. If you build
a bridge, control the operations of an aircraft carrier, or launch
a ballistic missile, you obey inflexible laws of knowledge and
technique. But the social techniques of manipulating pressure
groups, or dealing with people who want to live in one area
rather than another, or preventing the decline of urban centres,
are essentially different from the techniques we can apply to the
control of material objects. The more we try to manipulate
societies, the more we lay ourselves open to Marcuse's other
line of criticism, which deals with the 'alienation' of all individuals in a rationalized society. This brings me on to the most
popular theme of the social criticism which was voiced in May.
It is not new, but rejuvenated. Modern society inflicts a kind of
'alienation' on all the individuals who comprise that society.

'Alienation' is an extraordinarily vague word to which various authors give three, four or even five meanings. But its common usage means roughly this: man feels himself a stranger in the world he inhabits, a slave to the organization to which he belongs. At this point we reach the line of criticism which has perhaps the greatest moral or intellectual resonance.

Let us start by considering plain facts. In any large-scale organization, the majority of the workers are cogs in the machine. The man working at his machine on a production line is only vaguely aware of the place of his individual job in the whole production process. We are concerned here with old ideas which have suddenly acquired a new immediacy. What proportion of workers in an anonymous mechanism are integrated, what proportion alienated? There are enormous differences according to the level in the hierarchy and the kind of work they are engaged in. The iniquities of the rationalization of industry have been realized and criticized for many years, but there has been little attempt to compare the lot of the worker at the lowest point of the hierarchy now and twenty or fifty years ago. In effect, society is still based on work which is almost servile in the sense that there is no true fulfilment to be found in it. The supreme injustice is that the most tedious jobs, the jobs for which the least skills are required, are the least well paid. The P.D.G.'s enjoy both the highest salaries and the most interesting life. The same is true in every society we know.

Yet there were many people in the junior management of industry who felt a kind of frustration which was not implicit in the nature of their work. And so we come back to a point I have already touched on, namely the reorganization of firms so as to increase the number of autonomous decision-making centres, to produce a free flow of information, and to remove the arbitrary, one might almost say magical elements given to some types of authority by position in the hierarchy.

Modernity does not exclude egalitarian personal relationships outside the hierarchy of authority.

The French model is unlike the American. The Americans make an effort to create at least the appearance of equality outside the authoritarian hierarchy. The desecration of that staff common-room is a symbol of the respect mingled with resentment which the students felt for people whom they should have considered merely as equals, who happened to have rather greater knowledge or to be a little less ignorant. University teachers who tried to establish a dialogue with their students were not always able to make the kind of contact they wanted, whereas they had not the slightest difficulty in doing so with foreign students whether in France or abroad.

Was the May revolution an effective way of modifying human relations within the University and in industry? What will the return to reality mean to people who have dreamt their dream of brotherhood, which was the negation of the hierarchy they knew, and their dream of total freedom, which was the negation of the oppressive rationality they had experienced?

A.D.   There was at least one question which occurred to me as you were talking. Do you think that the obviously bad relationships which exists between teachers and students, and workers and bosses, could be due at least in part to the French educational system and to the way in which young children are brought up? Some English and American sociologists seem to have thought so.

R.A.   You are thinking of Wylie. Yes, Anglo-Saxon observers see the authoritarian relationship between teachers and pupils, established often as early as the primary school, as a feature of French education. Some have the impression that this authoritarianism has become less marked over recent years. From another point of view, no young generation has ever had so much freedom within the family, especially the bourgeois family, as the generation which has just revolted. I do not feel able to formulate any valid opinions on the subtle relationship between greater freedom within the family and the continuation of an authoritarian relationship in the primary school and sometimes in the secondary school. Even if the American authors are right, this traditional style of education is not the explanation of the recent unusual phenomena. But it is true that if children had grown used, right from the primary school, or at least from the start of secondary school, to the principle of organizing themselves and submitting to their own discipline, and of dis- cussing public affairs in a rational way, the politicization of the senior classes would have taken on a different form.

There are many aspects of French secondary education which I find perturbing apart from the authoritarian pupil-teacher relationship. I am concerned, for instance, about the emphasis placed on abstract, rhetorical forms of education to the detriment of others. People are surprised when 20-year-olds want to rebuild society. Yet when they were 15 they were being required to discuss Racine's attitude to love; at 17, after three months in the top class they were writing refutations of Kantian philosophy. There is a kind of general culture which is dear to many of my colleagues, which consists of nothing but the art of holding forth agreeably about things one knows nothing about. Some critics of this form of education claim that it puts children from the working class at a disadvantage, but this is far from being its only consequence. There is not a great deal of difference —apart from the standard of talent for rhetoric—between the 15-year-old schoolboy analyzing attitudes to love in the works of Racine and the 20-year-old student in the *École Normale* who interprets *Das Kapital* without having read Ricardo[1] and with no knowledge of the way a modern economy operates. Many higher intellectuals have an incredible scorn for facts. The formula 'there are no facts' is much acclaimed in Parisian circles. Of course, I am aware that in a sense this formula is philosophically true. There are no facts which have not been constructed —what a physician regards as a fact exists as such only within an intellectual system which has been created by science. As far as history is concerned, facts are either observed or reconstructed from documents by an historian. I am aware of this kind of consideration—after all, I began my career as a philosopher by making speculations of this kind. But when all is said and done at times I am tempted to turn Beotian and state that every society is subject to the constraints of fact—the need for production, for organization, for a technical hierarchy, the need for a techno-bureaucracy and so on. French intellectuals are so subtle that they end up by forgetting the obvious.

Whatever its faults, the French school has an extraordinary power of forcing assimilation. The son of any émigré from central or southern Europe who follows a full-time course in a *lycée* becomes French in his attitudes, his qualities and his faults.

The French system has the power to *denationalize*, to erase an immigrant's original tradition. The American system, on the other hand, superimposes typically American values and behaviour patterns on the cultural background of immigrants. But the French system has one great weakness—it creates intellectuals rather than citizens. Many products of the French educational system emerge with great admiration for French culture and extreme scorn for French political institutions. Respect for the French University has survived French rule in countries which were under French dominion for long periods. Many people who have been educated at the Sorbonne have gone on resisting American influence because they have preserved a proud memory of their teachers and of our system. This said, maybe the May revolutionaries will end up by convincing them of the stupidity of our professors, and our former pupils will conclude that their fondness for our system is misplaced, and will try to reorientate themselves not towards Cuban or Soviet culture, but towards American culture, which would be a logical, rather than a paradoxical result of the anti-Americanism of our intellectuals.

A.D.   You have used the words 'participation' and 'intelligentsia'. Perhaps at this point you could draw some conclusions in some areas from what you have just been analyzing.

R.A.   I use the word 'participation' with some reluctance because it is now on everybody's lips. A word which can be used in every sense no longer has any sense at all.

As far as the President of the Republic was concerned, he merely began to use his opponents' favourite word—'participation'—in place of his own favourite word—'association'. This concept reveals a certain yearning, but does not define any programme of action. It expresses a longing, which a great many French people share, to be treated as human beings and not as objects like raw materials or the cogs in a machine. People aspire to dignity, to the status of a subject. Who would oppose these aspirations? The question is, how can they be satisfied? At some levels, the only conceivable way involves a transformation in personal relationships. At others, there is a desire for representation on management committees—by direct participation in the case of small units, or by delegates in the case of larger organizations; but there again I have much greater faith in the reform of the organization itself than in the power of constitutions. Unfortunately, in the University especially, the result of 'participation' seems to be the establishment of representative institutions rather like the parliamentary assemblies of the past, rather than any fundamental transformation of the teacher-student relationship.

Let us take an example: the election of professors by the Assembly of the Faculty of Letters in the University of Paris. This kind of election was absurd even when the Assembly was made up exclusively of professors. Why? There were about 150 professors in the Faculty. On 'major election' days—which can be compared to important days in Parliament—more than two-thirds of the professors attended the Assembly. Normally less than 10 per cent of the electors knew anything of the academic merits of the candidates, and fewer still could appreciate their skills as teachers. When elections were contested, the debates were like a series of funeral orations or academic eulogies. If *assistants* and *maîtres-assistants* were to sit in the Assemblies as well, the Assemblies would become even more monstrous. If this were to happen, the result of 'participation' would have to be a devaluation of the Assembly and the creation of *ad hoc* electoral committees which would include *assistants* and *maîtres-assistants*, but which would be small enough to make a genuine attempt to find the best candidate.

In these circumstances, 'participation' would therefore tend to replace direct democracy (election by the whole Assembly) with a two-tier democracy, with election being put in the hands of a committee or competent persons removed as far as possible from pressure groups.

The same thing would happen in industry or in society as a whole. No-one knows the miraculous formula which would rid men, in their everyday lives, of the pressures of a semi-rational system, with all its inequalities, which obeys no one and which imposes itself on everyone.

General de Gaulle presents his philosophy in dialectical form. He rejects capitalism—thesis—which entails the class struggle, proletariat versus bourgeoisie, workers versus employers. He condemns communism—antithesis—which uses force and despotism to create a factitious unity. Beyond these two—synthesis —there is 'association' or 'participation'. But as far as I know, General de Gaulle has never said of what it is that association or participation consists. The philosophy of association or participation is a reflection of social ideas which were in favour among the Catholic bourgeoisie of Northern France at the start of the twentieth century. There are many factors which inhibit the development of this philosophy into institutions. Last year experts explained that profit-sharing has many risks as long as self financing remains a major condition of economic progress. How can industrial firms operating on narrow profit margins be deprived of a substantial part of their profit, gross or net, without a consequent deceleration in growth? Despite what one famous plan says, annual reinvestment does not in itself represent an increase in the value of a firm's assets since re-investment merely makes it possible to maintain the value of existing plant. These have a value only in as far as they can produce at a competitive price. The idea of the redistribution of capital by means of re-investment is based on a fundamental error. In some countries, especially the United States, reinvestment of profits tends to produce a progressive increase in the value of assets, while in other countries and in other circumstances, reinvestment of profits is only enough to avoid the decline in value of assets. Perhaps General de Gaulle will go beyond profit-sharing and follow the ideas of M. Capitant or of M. Bloch-Lainé.[2] I have great personal respect and sympathy for M. Bloch-Lainé, but I have hardly any faith at all in his ideas for the reform of industry. I am afraid that industry might be brought to the same state as was produced in the universities during the weeks of strikes and revolution. I am equally sceptical in both cases. I am all in favour of a progressive reorganization of industry which would make junior management feel that it was no longer excluded, but control committees which would say yes or no, which would vote for or against management decisions, the introduction into industry of representative democracy or rule by assembly, all this seems to me to be fraught with danger for the economy and for the country. The May madness ended in a kind of farce. General de Gaulle, no lover of parliaments or of dialogue, appeared to be going to impose dialogue and representation on everyone. If there is one institution which is by nature unsuited to the spirit of parliamentarianism, that institution is the industrial concern.

I personally feel that the National Assembly has an indispensable function to fulfil. I also approve of the idea that students and teachers should be represented in the management of the University. I do not, however, believe that there is any constitutional formula which can turn the dream of participation into reality either in industry or in the University. You may feel that I am being pessimistic. After innumerable constitutional experiments, the French people have realized the futility of the search for a miraculous text which would guarantee peace and efficiency. Let us give the text of the constitution a chance to last for a time, and eventually, because of its endurance, it might begin to gain our respect. Our legislators may be able to formulate some portmanteau law on participation in industry, but it must be couched in sufficiently vague and general terms to tolerate widely varying practices depending on individual circumstances and on the demands of international competition. Because of the events of May most French firms will show no profit this year. If things turn out badly, 80 per cent of them will lose money. In such a situation, legislation for industry based on Capitant's ideas would make a much more serious crisis inevitable. The consequences of the pseudo-revolution of May would be supplemented by the serious short-term results of a legislative revolution, which would be as dire for the economy as those of the revolution of the barricades.

A.D.   I am not sure whether M. Bloch-Lainé, for whom I share your respect, would sum up his reform proposals for industry as being the management of an industrial concern by an assembly set up within it.

R.A.   You are right. That was an unfair over-simplification. After all, I have told M. Bloch-Lainé that I am one of his admirers. I said to him 'The action you have taken in many fields has been that of a boss with a power which puts the power of bosses in the private sector in the shade.' M. Bloch-Lainé was a technocrat in the best sense of the term, who seldom felt himself restricted by the advice he was given, who set very little store by the approval of his subordinates and who was very little subject to Government restraint. He is an example at the State level of the big industrialist, who in every modern economy is the mainstay of the strength of industry and the prosperity of the nation. One day I asked him whether he himself would accept the limitation of authority which he proposed to impose on his colleagues in the private sector. You may be about to reply that senior officials are appointed by the State, while directors of firms in private industry are either co-opted to the board or inherit their seats; at the same time, private enterprise firms have to make profits, while in principle the directors of major public undertakings do not. In firms in the para-public sector, however, many directors, former civil servants, are in a financial situation comparable to that of private industry, and they are no more willing to submit to committee decisions than are the directors of private enterprise firms. It is true that senior officials in the public sector are appointed by politicians. But is this any absolute guarantee of their competence?

In the private sector there is a risk that the rights of inheritance will put the power of management into unqualified hands. In the more modern sectors of industry this happens less and less often. The heir who lacks the necessary qualities retains a well-paid position, but leaves the real power to others. This substitution of choice for inheritance is a daily occurrence. All that remains to establish is whether the various proposed methods of submitting this choice or other managerial decisions to the vote of an assembly in which staff or workers are represented, would result in an improvement in the quality of the choice or the efficiency of management, and would lead to employees having a real feeling of participation. While I shall give no outright answer to any of these questions, I have my doubts.

A.D.   Would I be distorting your thought if I were to say that basically you would like to see a more rational approach to industrial management, a better flow of information within the firm—which might mean that the flow of information might become more formalized or less—and finally a modification in the manner of relationships which would not affect decision making but which would have an effect on the formal hierarchical structure?

R.A.   Two precise points. I would like to see industrial managers making the practice of specific authority based on competence and responsibility a much more integral part of their working relationships, and laying less emphasis on statutory superiority. It is essential for the modernization of the French economy that there should be a feeling of participation, but this will not result from portmanteau legislation or from constitutions framed by lawyers which rapidly fall into disuse. The only possibility is a continuous process of creation; to ensure prosperity and unity, the firm must have at least a minimum of community feeling. This feeling cannot exist unless the top man manages to associate his colleagues, his junior managers, his clerical and manual workers with the life of the firm. He can do this either by means of meetings where he can hand on information, or by a kind of fluidity in management. In industry and in the State alike, new constitutions start off by administering a jolt, and then wear out without having served their purpose. If industrialists do not want constitutions, constitutions will not work. But if they have understood the lessons of May, this difficult and progressive transformation will be effected whether there are constitutions or not.

I am thinking of one firm with incomparably high technical standards which has preserved a paternalist tradition, and which established relations with the trade unions for the third time in fifty years during the events of May. In some cases the slogan 'the workers are fighting for their dignity', often pure demagogy, has a real meaning. The mass of workers see discussion on an equal footing between management and unions as the symbol of their dignity. No matter what wages are offered, no matter what social advantages are available, there is a certain kind of management which is no longer acceptable to the workers. And that is a good thing.

A.D.   So you have drawn one lesson from the University and another from industry. I think you may have conclusions to draw from two other fields—from the intelligentsia and the political society of France.

R.A.   Let us start with the political society. Whether we like it or not, whether we see it as a matter for self congratulation or for regret, France is entering on a kind of government which you and I would call government by a dominant party, or a hegemony. It is not a one-party system. Opposition parties exist, and intellectual and personal freedoms are respected. But one party has an overwhelming majority, and the opposition parties are so divided that no one can see any possibility of the majority party being replaced in power. In India the Congress Party has been dominant since independence, and there has been no suppression of liberties. In my lecture courses I have always spent some time on dominant party régimes which I include in the category of pluralist democracies and not in that of single-party systems. Yet in France the predominance of one party which, failing revolution, can be certain of being in power for some years to come is not without its dangers. The May explosion, even if its direct target was not General de Gaulle or Gaullism, showed a widespread and profound dissatisfaction with existing society. (Maybe the fact that no one was killed was largely due to the abstract nature of the enemy under attack.) The Gaullist régime was part of the system which was under fire, and it had aggravated the intrinsic faults of the French administrative and social order. There were few parliamentary debates, no safety valves, a large number of ministers were former civil servants and had retained their civil service authoritarian approach. The Gaullist régime convinced me of the value of having ministers who act in what we call the republican style. When a bureaucracy is as centralized and as hierarchically controlled as ours, it will not become a decentralized, non-authoritarian system overnight; Alain[3] was therefore quite right to say that the politician who represents his constituents against the authority of Paris is playing a vital rôle. In the long run the French are not the people to accept a symbolically tough Government. They want men who are aware of their grievances, even unjustified grievances, and who temper the inflexibility of government with a concern for individual interests, even if those interests do not always seem to merit respect from a man who is committed to the collective interest alone. I had some faint hope that the new Gaullism would accept one of the lessons of the May explosion. Not only the economic lesson—that the country must not be exposed to a pressure greater than that which the majority of the French people are prepared to tolerate—but a political lesson, that no impression must be given that power and the benefits of power are in the hands of a monopoly.

The French people must not be treated with disdain, and with a disdain which becomes even more haughty, the more the leaders claim to love France. Those who are not directly represented in the party in power must not be ignored. Non-Gaullist Frenchmen must be treated and addressed as if they are just as good Frenchmen as the others. The Gaullists infuriated many non-Gaullists less by what they did than the way they did it. Of course General de Gaulle will never change his personal style but no matter how much it may hurt some ex-*Action Française*[4] doctrinaires, if tomorrow's Gaullism wishes to survive de Gaulle, it will have to learn, or re-learn, a language which is acceptable to non-Gaullists and anti-Gaullists. The Gaullists must allow people who do not belong to this strange dominant party to have some participation in regional and other administration. The dominant party almost crumbled in May, and the mad rush of events restored it in a spectacular way to a power which it had never previously enjoyed. The party has some extraordinary characteristics. It has no doctrine, and has never had one. Its first success came in 1958 under the banner of 'Algerie Française', and it then went on to watch over Algeria's independence. It gathers its votes from traditional France and from a normally left-inclined electoral fringe, and yet its foreign policy is the closest to that which could be desired by the Communist Party or the Soviet Union. It could be, that tomorrow, if General de Gaulle so wished it—and he would certainly derive some sombre pleasure from it—a law could be passed to complete the ruin of private enterprise, which M. Mendès-France, who is less ignorant of economics, would have spared in the national interest. It is a strange hegemonic party, which during his presidency at least has been entirely subject to the will of one man, who wants a revolution which is ill defined, but which he wants passionately. It is a party of hegemony which has made opposition difficult since the President of the Republic has laid down once and for all that the Government and the majority are his and his alone. It is impossible to challenge the Government or the parliament without challenging the President of the Republic himself. If France is to remain a liberal democratic country untroubled by explosions and civil war, the party of hegemony will not only have to tame and master its victory, but it will also have to change its style and its methods of operation. It was not going the right way about it with M. Couve de Murville and his crew. That was not the team to introduce traditions of dialogue and communication derived from the despised third and fourth republics into its system of bureaucratic authoritarianism, stretching as it does, right up to ministerial level.

The old ministerial crises were less costly than a crisis like that of May.

While there is no need to expect a new major crisis to erupt again soon, we now know that the façade of order conceals a potential for revolt whose power is clearly visible even to the greatest sceptics. I persist in my belief that the May events were a psychodrama rather than a real drama, and a revolutionary comedy rather than a revolution. Yet the way in which the strikes spread, and the public's uncertainty about the resistance offered by the Government, were psychological realities. They may have been illusions, but illusions which are shared by all tend to become confused with reality.

Everyone talks about putting a revolution to good use. The Gaullist Party should have set about reforming itself, after its electoral triumph, in much the same way that it would have been obliged to do if it had been confronted with an opposition capable of forming an alternative government. It now finds itself with apparently less need to reform itself than it would have if the events had never taken place. Had there been no May revolution, the Gaullists would have had to face the threat of a semi-revolt by the Independents, the possible attraction of the centre, and the possibility of a left-wing candidate being elected at the second round of voting over a moderate. The Communist Party no longer inspired fear in the country, and M. Mitterand, or his successor, had a chance within a few per cent of being elected President. All these possibilities have now melted like snow in the sun, the sun of May. General de Gaulle interpreted the crisis within the framework of his 'philosophy'. He hoped to overtake the revolutionaries on their left in the same way that the P.S.U. hoped to overtake the Communist Party. But he, like the P.S.U., has not succeeded.

The threat of revolt exists, but if the aim is to overthrow the Government by force, real force must be used. The symbol of force is only enough to overthrow a government which is on the way out already. I do not think that the adventure can be repeated again in the near future, but this time using real force. Perhaps I am being led into error by over-optimism. Gaullism is solidly ensconced in power with no parliamentary opposition. It has nothing to fear except splits, the ideas of General de Gaulle himself, and the material consequences of the May crisis. Since there is no possible alternative government, Gaullism is being asked to become a government for the whole of the French people. To do so it must not rely on some miraculous recipe of participation, but must change its style, and make itself available to a dialogue. So much for the first point.

The second point you mentioned was the intelligentsia. I find some embarrassment in talking about my intellectual colleagues because I inspire such violent hostility in some of them that I would not wish to imitate them and reply to them in kind.

There was another period when orthodox intellectuals (by which I mean the intelligentsia of the left) put me in quarantine. That was from 1946 or 1947 to 1955 or 1956, during the great debate between the pro-Communist (or pro-Soviet) faction and those who were in favour of the Atlantic Community. I came out of quarantine not because I managed to persuade anyone over to my way of thinking, but because of Khrushchev's speech. After all, if I had known in 1955 that in 1956 Khrushchev was going to make a speech about the crimes of Stalinism, I might not have bothered to write *The Opium of the Intellectuals*. After the event I feel that I have spent too much time in debates of limited academic range, and whose political effectiveness was also unfortunately small. Most men, and above all intellectuals, believe what they want to believe, once and for all, I perhaps included, and in the last analysis they make statements of faith which are totally immune to argument.

So I was delivered from solitude by Khrushchev's speech, and for several years my views on Algeria and my comparative analyses of Soviet and Western industrial societies corresponded to a state of mind in others which was sufficiently widespread to offer me a certain audience in circles which ten years earlier had rejected me absolutely. This time I will be even more harshly condemned by the left. My articles on the University crisis have brought me enthusiastic support from colleagues who are far from being on the right, and there are several intellectuals and professors from the left who shared my reaction to the violation of the moral code of the University. But my attitude has brought down on me the passionate and impassioned hostility of the orthodox left (and I have done my best to deserve it).

According to reports by friends who move in all sorts of circles, the severest criticism is not directed at my hostility to the

University revolution: many people believe that I was bound to be hostile to it despite my criticisms of the traditional University. These people expected ironically, or merely with indifference, that I would react as I did. Perhaps I reacted with more heat than they thought I had, but after all in May and June, heat and passion were the commonest things in the world.

A number of moderates who sympathized with the revolution to a greater or lesser extent have turned against me because of what they regard as my contempt for the events of May. They are furious, almost beside themselves because I do not take the students, the teachers and the intellectuals, the actors in this revolutionary comedy, seriously enough. Many friends or former friends, who on the whole agree with my judgments, disagree with me when I talk of carnivals or masquerades, and when I show myself to be more a sceptic than an admirer of these events. I refuse to salute our 'admirable youth'. Too many grown men have done so. Barricades which are symbolically effective seem to me to be neither an intellectual nor a moral achievement. If young people have some exalted memory of the barricades, well and good. Why should old people be obliged to counterfeit sentiments which they do not feel? If the young denounce the brutality of the C.R.S. while in the same breath preaching the cult of violence themselves, the contradiction seems to me to be nothing more than a good technique of subversion. But men of my generation or of the generation after do not want to feel that they were caught up in what I persist in calling collective madness. They do not accept that they lost their self-control and that for a few weeks or a few days they were out of their minds. I admit I was out of mine for two days between the Billancourt rejection of the Grenelle agreements and General de Gaulle's speech. During that time I wondered whether the President of the Republic had really lost control of the situation, and if a régime which was based on one man's magic was going to collapse the moment that that magic vanished. We now know that on Wednesday 29th May M. Pompidou himself was not certain that General de Gaulle was going to come back.

Many professors and intellectuals hold that the May revolution marks a major historical date. Malraux himself, after all, must believe so, since he spoke of it as the end of a world. I have no intention of prophesying: a civilization with a Church which is in a state of self-doubt, and which sometimes denies its own validity, a civilization shorn of patriotic and traditional values, may well be in the last stages before death. A society which depends on the voluntary co-operation of millions upon millions of individuals in rationalized organizations runs the risk of being paralysed by the violence of the minority or the disaffection of the majority. Perhaps the events of May will be seen in the future as an indication of the basic precariousness of a liberal order in a scientific civilization. I do not say categorically that those who admire the May revolution are wrong. Maybe the future will prove them right, and historians will see that what appears to me to have been a revolutionary comedy was in fact a manifestation of the outburst of subterranean destructive forces. But even if all this should be so, these revolutionaries who dream of establishing direct democracy in an industrial society are out of their minds. The grievances which were held against the government in power had nothing to do with the course the events took. The May crisis developed in a way similar to the crisis of 1848, but more absurdly, and I claim the right to be as severe in my criticism of the events of May 1968 as the socialist Proudhon, the liberal Tocqueville and Karl Marx were in theirs of the imitators of the Great Revolution, the comedians of 1848. Why should we admire these pseudo-Jacobin clubs where pseudo-revolutionaries held interminable discussions about pseudo-reforms? Why should we admire professors of constitutional law who violate legality and find pseudo-justifications for pseudo-revolutionary structures, for constitutions full of pseudo-innovations, and which could not possibly operate? I refuse to recognize 'Byzantine' intellectuals who express themselves in language incomprehensible to common mortals, and who set themselves up as ringleaders of a revolution in the mid-twentieth century, as the interpreters of the people or the proletariat or even of the students themselves. And nothing will dissuade me

123

from my view that the storming of the Hotel Massa by the progressive writers and the revolution of successful film directors at the Cannes festival were symbolic of a period which was rich in absurd episodes. These two seem to me to be actions typical of a certain kind of Paris intelligentsia which mixes 'Byzantinism' with Castroism or Maoism. In 1961 I found the Cuban revolution to be pretty inefficient but agreeable enough for the sugar cane island. Probably most of the people of Cuba are happier under Fidel than they were under the previous régime. I do not believe that the Cuban revolution was a great event in universal history, and anyway the French people would have no use for this kind of revolution. As for the Chinese revolution, I know very little about it, like most of those who talk about it (or do *not* talk about it), and the idea of bringing to the Sorbonne the *impression* which we have of the Chinese revolution seems to me to be entirely worthy of the intellectuals of Paris. It is wholly unreasonable, but its consequences may ultimately prove to be disastrous.

The real, major intellectuals, and even the less real and less major, will continue to despise me for not falling in with the game, for not currying popularity by flattering youth and paying homage to fashionable ideas. I still see the May events as a gloomy period in the history of France. No one came out of it any better off, and no one has any valid reason for being proud of it.

All well-accredited intellectuals make patronizing comments about the way the French people voted for de Gaulle, while I, although I am far from being a Gaullist, think that this vote was predictable, inevitable and not unreasonable. Who else could the French people have voted for?

You see that I am overstating my case. I decided to overstate it because too many people who in their heart of hearts agree with me are afraid to say so out loud.

I was bored by Godard's film *Week-end*, yet in a way this film was prophetic. The Seine-et-Oise Liberation Committee which appears briefly in the film almost existed in reality. The deliberate absurdity of Godard's film was a kind of advance reflection of the absurdity of the events of May. The film perhaps ceased to be absurd when the events brought it to life, but the events took on the absurdity which I found in the film.

What can one do in a country where one of the most important bodies of people—the glory-laden intellectuals—admire nothing but destruction, without having any conception of an order which might be able to replace the one they want to destroy? I have no answer. Intellectuals normally have a critical function. After all, I have always been a ready critic of French governments to such an extent that I cannot be accused of conformism or of servility to government, but the critical function becomes sheer nihilism when it produces an absolute condemnation of society, without advancing any idea of an alternative society, when it preaches the cult of pure violence.

At the beginning of the student movement, some major intellectuals, signed a resolution. I have forgotten its exact terms, but the sense was this: keep on saying *no*, and above all do not be in too much of a hurry to formulate your credos and your aims. The god of the intellectuals of the sixties was no longer the Sartre who had dominated the post-war period, but a mixture of Lévi-Strauss,[5] Foucault,[6] Althusser[7] and Lacan.[8] All passed for structuralists, although they were structuralists in different ways. The most refined of the intelligentsia watched Godard's films, read Lacan without understanding him, and swore by the scientificism of Althusser and acclaimed Lévi-Strauss's structuralism. Oddly, some of these avant-garde intellectuals claimed to be scientific with respect to ethnology or economics, but Maoist when it came to action. During the May period the scientificism disappeared and the cult of action, the cult of the cultural revolution spread in various forms. Sartre and *Dialectical Reason*, the *groupe en fusion*, the revolutionary mob, had taken their revenge on the structure of society.

The intelligentsia's systematic criticism of the liberal society ends up by weakening and undermining a very fragile order. This kind of criticism tends to induce a guilty conscience in the responsible members of society, and particularly in their children. Now, while no ruling class rules entirely innocently, a ruling class which is uncertain of itself condemns itself to death. The manager of a private firm who does not believe in the firm has abdicated in advance, and will yield at the first blow. The vague, emotional leftism of the intelligentsia won the support of well intentioned people and of their children. Very probably the uneasy conscience of those in authority was one of the reasons for the decomposition which we saw in May. I am all in favour of giving the leaders of society a guilty conscience for not having done their job properly, either by failing to exert proper control and leadership or by failing to create a climate of cooperation. But to reject one social order without having any notion of the order which might be erected in its place is bound to entail misery for everyone.

Again, the educational system, right from the primary schools to the Sorbonne, has an absolutely vital rôle to play—the education of those who in the future will be filling crucial positions in society. If our schools and universities disseminate a revolutionary ideology, whether it be Communist or nihilist they will be creating a permanent tension between the social rôle of these graduates of the future and their inner convictions. The privileged classes will escape from this contradiction by withdrawal and apathy, by retiring to their country cottages; they will not respond with a determination to build a modern France in which our real values can be safeguarded. These values derive from two ideals: liberalism and efficiency. These ideals, I agree, have been attained only imperfectly—but have they been realized any better in the Soviet Union or China? The glorification of the guerilla or of violence which we have seen in France in 1968 is nothing but the nihilism of the intellectuals.

I am in no way tempted to write a sequel to *The Opium of the Intellectuals* directed against today's Maoists or Castroites. Today's fashionable ideology is almost totally devoid of content. How can there be any real debate with an advocate of direct democracy in an industrial society? The only way is to invite him to visit any Soviet, British, American or French firm.

Possibly I attach too much importance to the rôle of the intelligentsia. Maybe France has a long and peaceful future ahead in which the paradox of a conservative people and revolutionary intellectuals will continue to exist. The former may find some compensation for their conservatism in the revolutionary word-spinning of the intellectuals, which at the same time will give these an opportunity to nurture a comforting disdain for their compatriots. Once more, the worst is not always certain to happen.

5

Summary Explanation
of an Absurd Episode

IF WE TAKE everything that happened in May 1968 together and
call it a revolution, the episode is bound to remain shrouded in
mystery. As I know from personal experience, outsiders are incapable of understanding how it was that a local students' revolt
(only a few hundred students initially) was able to develop into
a national crisis and make the régime totter despite the fact that
there was no revolutionary party or mass leader with any real
intention of taking over power. If we re-run the film sequence
by sequence, the feeling of mystification is gradually dissipated.

1. The university authorities, and later the Government,
reacted clumsily in the first instance to the initial student demonstrations. There was a similarly clumsy handling of almost every
other similar case everywhere in the world. University authorities, in France a dean elected by the professors or a rector appointed by the Government, or in America the regents, a president or a dean, feel themselves morally and materially defence-
less when confronted with students who apply the techniques of
opposition and subversion, whether or not the use of these techniques is conscious and deliberate. As soon as the students'
refusal to obey became provocative and collective, university
politics became politics of the street. The authorities inevitably

hesitated between the two alternative courses open to them —to allow lawlessness to continue, or to bring in an external force, the police—and they were justly accused of opting first for one alternative and then the other, and for having done so in each case at precisely the wrong time. A kind of 'age group solidarity', which normally is very diffuse, but which any crisis tends to strengthen, led a fairly considerable number of students to muster to the 'professional revolutionaries'. The teaching body was divided. Some of the students' demands were essentially legitimate in any circumstances. Even if they were excessive or debatable, an American liberal or a French leftist would maintain that they should have been met with dialogue, not with repression. Whether they were to win or lose the ringleaders would have achieved what they set out to achieve—they would have severely shaken an institution which depends on the voluntary self-discipline of all its members.

What happened in France is different from what happened at Berkeley and Columbia only in degree, not in scenario. As the Paris University authorities are almost entirely dependent on the ministry—to such a degree that they can take no serious decision without consultation—it was the University and Government together which suffered the backlash of the 'clumsy reactions' to the classic techniques of subversion. After a week the tide of propaganda was in full flood, police violence was monstrous, whereas the erection of the barricades by students, and some teachers, immediately found a niche in the popular imagination alongside similar exploits from the past. The foreign press and the fashionable suburbs admired these wild and glorious young people. The crisis, started off by a handful of students at Nanterre(100 to 150 activists, and a few hundred sympathizers) grew within a week into the Sorbonne Commune, and then gradually into the establishment of genuine student power, or a mixture of student-teacher power, in almost every institution of higher education. After another week, the movement began to spread into the *lycées*. It is not possible for the moment to establish how much of this resulted from contagion or spontaneous imitation, and how much was due to planned action by

activist minorities. Many reports suggest that in the case of the
lycées the decisive factor was the action of these minorities.

Outsiders may reluctantly accept that as a result of the concentration of the students and organizations in Paris the revolt
could spread to the whole University, having been limited initially to one or two establishments, but he will be amazed and
horrified by the fact that a large number of university teachers
took part in action directed against the very status of the teaching staff and against the university system. We cannot tell the
numerical strength of the various groups, but there were plenty
of teachers of all grades everywhere who gave an appearance of
legality to the committees set up to study reforms (these committees provided an honourable way of keeping students busy
in the absence of lectures and examinations) and also to the
plenary and general assemblies, which were essentially insurrectional by nature. There were very few rectors or deans who
consistently ried to maintain the rule of law through these weeks.

Why did these adults give in, why did the authorities capitulate? In the absence of analytical studies, which would anyway
probably be only of a limited value if they were to be carried
out so long after the event, everyone must decide for himself in
the light of his own experience and the way he feels, whether
the motives of the actors were noble or unworthy. Some teachers
who were inclined to the left in their private views suddenly
found themselves confronted with a movement which was comparable with other movements which they had praised in their
lectures. These lecture-hall revolutionaries were caught in a trap
of their own making—when the revolution spread to the lecture
hall, they had either to join it or to deny it. It is supremely
important to a man of the left to keep faith with his ill-defined
but sacred principles. The French universities revolted against
the stifling rule of the ministry, and when they did so the alliance between the teachers and the taught was transformed. The
teachers no longer humiliated themselves before the students,
they joined them, with the aim of wresting genuine authority
from the ministry (the equivalent of the Regents of Berkeley or
the Trustees of Columbia). The quarrel about the division of

power between students and teachers was inextricably linked with the other quarrel about the division of power between the administration and the faculty. The teaching body split into many groups according to age, status and career prospects. A shake up of the system might offer some teachers chances they had never even dreamed of. The hierarchy, too rigid, as always in France, collapsed, and so there was room for the illusion of equality to flourish. For three weeks the simplest and least dangerous course appeared to be non-resistance to the movement: liberal victors forgive, revolutionary victors do not. Perhaps many teachers had doubts deep within themselves about the legitimacy of their position, about the quality of the teaching they were giving, and about the University itself. Some of them, the revolutionaries, believed in the revolution, while others took part to foster personal ambition or because they doubted the validity of their profession. A collective capitulation even if it is imposed by a minority, suggests an uneasy collective conscience.

2. The second sequence—from the Sorbonne Commune to the occupation of the factories—is open to shades of interpretation. Was the spontaneous action of activist groups in the first two factories occupied, directly due to the Government's capitulation? Did the C.F.D.T. see this as a good opportunity to overtake the C.G.T. on the left? Did the pro-Chinese cells take the initiative? Whatever the causes, we know that the spread of strikes and the occupation of factories were the result of a C.G.T. decision, and that the C.G.T. wanted to regain control of its troops while making a new appearance in its rôle as the driving spirit of the workers' struggles.

True, here again, the speed with which the spark spread the fire can be understood only in the light of some peculiarly French characteristics—the anarcho-syndicalist temperament, the power of symbols like the red flag and the black flag, and the weakness of organized unions. The way in which the C.G.T. organized unofficial strikes and set up strike pickets makes it impossible to take the numbers of the strikers at their face value. At the start the Renault workers did not want to strike—this did not prevent their reluctantly accepting, however, after fifteen days' strike, a disappointing settlement, which set the seal on the futility of pseudo-revolution, which had been as costly for them as it was for the nation at large.

Could a similar phenomenon occur elsewhere? In the present state of our experience, we must answer 'no', but we can do so only with some hesitation. The revolutionary virus is still contagious. The establishment of 'Trotskyite' or 'Maoist' cells in Italian and West German factories will go on. In Italy, trade unions and workers are still Communist-dominated. Our neighbours and partners would be wrong to be reassured too easily, or to believe that French frivolity was the sole cause of this revolutionary comedy, which might so easily have been, and which still might be, a tragedy. Nor must we forget that the Communist Party does not give the Government its semi-co-operation for nothing: the diplomatic policies of the French Government, whether or not they are in the interests of France, are a source of considerable satisfaction to the men in the Kremlin. Italy and especially West Germany are neither able nor willing to pay this kind of price.

3. The third sequence is obviously the most mysterious. It can only be understood by those who lived through this period in Paris, and then only in general terms. This is the quasi disappearance of the legal authority of the State between General de Gaulle's return to Paris and his speech on 30th May. First the absence of the Prime Minister, and then that of General de Gaulle, prevented the Government from taking any coherent or determined action during the first weeks. When General de Gaulle returned, he seemed to be unable to get to grips with the events. At first he maintained a total silence, which he broke only to make a television appearance on 24th May, when he looked older and bitter. This behaviour alone was enough to reinforce the feeling already current in Paris that authority had abdicated and left a void.

At this point we come up against another specifically French characteristic, the way in which people have become accustomed to accept changes in the régime brought about by revolt and the way in which the average Frenchman, and even high officials, are prepared to accept new masters and the general decomposition of the hierarchy and of social bonds when the bureaucracy, the spinal column of France, breaks up. I think that France is the only modern state where society is so incapable of independent survival when the machinery of government ceases to function.

4. If we take these sequences one at a time, they seem to me to be fairly intelligible, but if we take them together, they powerfully stimulate the imagination, even if we force ourselves to look at the successive episodes in a matter-of-fact way. They were absurd, epic and bizarre in turn. The events rarely merited respect, and as they ran their course every national institution from the Presidency of the Republic to the national television and broadcasting system via the University and the press compromised themselves to the point of being partially discredited (certainly in the view of foreigners, if not in French eyes).

Neither Gaullists (who spoke of 'the end of a world') nor revolutionaries want to see these events debunked; both parties seek to justify their actions by raising the events to the level of universal history. The events are certainly significant if only as a symbol of the vulnerability of twentieth-century liberal France, and perhaps of every liberal society of this century. Maybe France's extreme sensibility amplifies an unease which affects the whole of Western civilization: what in other countries manifests itself as a brief feverish outburst, in France becomes, or seems to become, an acute crisis which puts the patient's life in jeopardy.

Since it has become fashionable for authors to quote their own works, I cite here a passage which I wrote in August 1963 as a preface to a series of lectures delivered in 1956–57 under the title 'The Class Struggle'. 'If we agree to describe as *pragmatic* the action which trade unions and political parties take with the aim of achieving reforms here and now (which Lenin described as trade-unionism on the English model), and to describe as *ideological* the action of the Communist Party in opposing the régime for the sake of opposing, and with a view to bringing

133

about revolution, we see that the progress made over the last fifteen years has strengthened the tendency towards pragmatism and weakened that towards ideology. But it would be wrong to conclude that from now on the only aim of social conflict will be to win "a larger slice of the cake", to obtain wage increases or to resist technical change which would involve painful retraining. Although it seems at the moment that the majority of workers in most countries have little interest in the various forms of worker participation in management, it is possible, and indeed probable, that in some countries we will see further demands for changes in the organization of industry. Lying between pragmatic argument and ideological conflict, there is a third kind of debate or struggle which will ultimately lead to an increase in workers' participation in industry, or in the participation of junior managers' or workers' representatives in some aspects of industrial managements.'

Although this demand was not the cause of the revolt either of the students, the workers or the junior managers, it was one of the major themes of the reforms which were worked out in the university committees, the committees in research institutes, and apparently in the committees of junior management in industry. General de Gaulle put his own favourite word 'association' in place of the word 'participation', without giving precise meaning to either idea. The workers, or at least the trade unions, still show the same indifference or contempt for this 'bourgeois trick'. But the intellectuals and the junior managerial staff appear to want increased participation in the control of laboratories universities and industrial firms, although it is not easy to differentiate between their various motives: there is a rejection of outside authority, a corporate desire to run their own affairs, a wish to see the taxpayers providing the cash and the university officials or the officials of research institutes spending it as they think best, and a legitimate desire—although one difficult to satisfy—to modify the organization of industry so as to associate unions and staff more closely with management.

The enthusiasm with which this demand has been taken up in France is due to the rôle of the intellectuals and the left-wing

Catholics. The C.F.D.T. used this as a weapon against the C.G.T. The revolutionaries inflated the demand for reforms which with certain reservations could have been achieved, into the old anarchist Utopia of workers' control. In his turn General de Gaulle tried to overtake the revolutionaries on their left by adopting the same slogan, which was more likely to complete the ruin of French industry than to transform the social order.

It is fairly easy to explain why France has played such an avant-garde rôle in this process. As far as politics and social questions are concerned, the French still prefer abstract ideas to facts. Their egalitarian anarchist dreams compensate for the rigidity of French institutions. And apart from this they also keep up their old habits of drawing up constitutions aimed at changing social behaviour, and of improvising on the spur of the moment reforms which have no chance of success unless given time and patience.

The fact remains that when the C.G.T.-dominated unions seemed at least to have been converted to pragmatism, the revolutionary movements rose up on the left of the Communist Party as if the hope of revolution had been moribund for a few years and was now being reborn in another form. Stalin was replaced by Mao, and the history of the Communist Party by the little red book. Once again high-ranking intellectuals threw up their hands in delight at a nursery-school reader. Once again it falls to France, and particularly to the extraordinary intellectuals of Paris,—those obscurantist 'in-group' writers, Jean-Luc Godard, linguists and structuralists, brilliant graduates and drop-outs from the meritocracy, verbal subtlety and the cult of violence—it falls to France to make the running and to act out as a kind of real-life comedy, the absurd world dreamt of by fashionable writers.

Every country has a small but virulent group of students who revolt against the establishment, against people of 35 almost as much against those of 60. Let us assume for the sake of argument that when Czechoslovak students demand liberty, they are doing just the same as German, American or French students who are fans of Mao or Fidel Castro. Let us allow that there may be some relationship between students from eastern Europe who demand liberties which they are refused, and students from the West who are aware that the liberties they have will not be able to change the world. France has given an extreme expression to a generation conflict which is sharper in the middle class than in the working class.

I am indeed particularly forcibly struck by the gap which has opened, at least within the University, between the generation born between 1945 and 1950 and earlier generations, which is much more remarkable than the gap which separates the over-thirties and the over-fifties. The young people of the middle class, whose parents are indifferent or over-indulgent, are released from all sexual, patriotic or traditional taboos, and they accept the benefits of the consumer society with no pangs of conscience, while denouncing the materialistic civilization in which most of the working class or the lower middle class, would like a greater share. To condemn this state of mind is as pointless as to admire it. No one can be really sure what its causes are—an abnormal condition of young adults whose existence has for too long been marginal or even childish in a sense, their unfulfilled need for a crusade, the lack of any causes to be embraced, the spiritual void of a privileged class which has had no restrictive yoke to shake off, no parents to oppose, no obstacles to overcome, and which finds allies among other young people who have reached the lowest echelons of the intellectual hierarchy at the expense of great effort and difficulty, and who are now bitter about a system which is too closed, too hierarchical, and too inegalitarian (even though this inequality is the result of competition). Some people have described this as a revolution of drop-outs, and they are very far from being right. It is a revolution of drop-outs and of the most brilliant minds, some disgusted in advance by a career which is already mapped out for them, others in revolt against a defeat they have already suffered. These elements were united yesterday against a society which seemed to be immovable, and united today by their memories of their futile fraternity and their shortlived triumph. They overcame the Bastille of the Sorbonne, and they rocked the Bastille of the Elysée. But they did not know, and they still do not know how to use the victory which might have been theirs. Of course, some of them will take their seats on university committees, and they will soon discover the frustration and boredom of committee work from which our colleagues in Britain and the United States already suffer. But the others, the extremists, the *enragés*, the nihilists are afraid that reforms may make revolution unnecessary. They may be able to paralyze the universities for several years to come. Sooner or later the sheep will themselves become *enragés*, and some government will eventually summon up the courage to wipe out the real causes of trouble.

The consumer society, or the producer society if you prefer, does not of itself provide any motive for living. Neither do penury or poverty. Lawmakers cannot cure boredom and frustration and the difficulty of living, nor can participation in university assemblies or industrial unions. Will the French people become any happier by partially sacrificing efficiency of control and setting up various forms of self-management or participation? I hope so, but I doubt it. In this we are far removed from the 'possessed' and the metaphysics of the guerillas.

5. Will the consequences of the events create a revolutionary situation which did not exist in April, but which the combination of events created in May? I am doubtful about this.

The Gaullists, with the approval of some constitutional lawyers, wanted to force a two-party system on France. They seem to have succeeded. As one of the parties or blocks is Communist-dominated, and as the mass of the French people are still afraid of Communism, the logical development of such a system is the establishment of a party of hegemony, with no alternative government. Fortunately the party of hegemony has a coherence which is only factitious, and which in all probability will not survive the charismatic figure on whom it depends. Even during General de Gaulle's lifetime, the party has only obeyed its leader out of habit, and because it was unaware of its own power. On 30th May in the Champs Élysées, it was not all the people of Paris who shouted 'Vive de Gaulle', and not everybody voted for him on 23rd and 30th June. The President of the

137

Republic needed the Union pour la Défense de la République[9] more than it needed him. But neither the General nor the party were aware of this.

In his television interview with Michel Droit, General de Gaulle did not abandon a single one of his favourite ideas, not even the independence of Quebec, on the eve of a General Election which returned to power a French-speaking Canadian, who is opposed to the idea of separatism. The combination of a foreign policy based on opposition to the United States and to Western solidarity, and a domestic policy based on opposition to the Communist Party, in the past described as separatist and today described as totalitarian, will form an explosive mixture in the future just as it did in the past. Gaullist philosophy has refused to recognize the reciprocal implications of these foreign and domestic policies. The double Gaullist-Communist game will go on. The Gaullists tolerate, without necessarily approving, propaganda on behalf of the revolutionaries of the third world, and they tolerate, too, progressives and Communists taking positions in both the private and public sectors. The Communists denounce 'personal power' without having any intention of overthrowing it, and with a long-term aim in mind. There is nothing to suggest that General de Gaulle has altered his order of priorities, with domestic matters still being subordinate to his 'grand design'. (In the past this irritated foreigners—in the future it will make them smile.) There is nothing to suggest that from now on he will agree to a dialogue, that he will allow directives to make way for discussion, that he has the slightest doubt of his own infinite wisdom, or that he has any greater respect for the French people, either for those who support him or those who do not.

Yet there will be something new. This man who listened to no one suddenly wished to issue a decree from on high to force all Frenchmen (except himself and Parliament) to engage in a permanent debate within each organization. The French people are to be obliged to participate in everything except the commands of the Prince.

No one can forecast where the formula of association between capital and labour on the 1968 model will end. In 1967 the Vallon amendment, after having kept economists worried for two years, finally led to a profit-sharing law which was largely derisory because, as a result of the operation of tax laws, the State found itself paying the share of the profit allocated to the workers. This time General de Gaulle, strengthened in his conviction that the establishment of an unprecedented economic and social system would be the crowning glory of his life's work, will not let himself be so easily stopped by his advisers, although these men, in as far as they think at all, are in private as outspoken about participation as is M. Pompidou. M. Pompidou, M. Michel Debré or M. Giscard d'Estaing could between them paralyse the first magistrate of the Republic if they were really determined to do so. Of course they will leave M. Couve de Murville and his collaborators to cope with the economic crisis which will be made worse by the hugely ambitious programmes of reform. Who will invest capital in industrial firms with inadequate profit margins, and whose legal status and basis will for months be subject to the arbitrary decisions of one omnipotent and incompetent man?

In terms of production per head of population, France is at roughly the same level as West Germany or Britain. But this does not hold good for the industrial product per head. In 1965 there were only 7·9 million workers in industry in France against 12 million in Britain and 13·2 million in West Germany. The proportion of workers engaged in industry was respectively 41, 47·5 and 50 per cent of the working population as a whole. Statistical studies show that the productivity of French industry is no worse than that of our two principal European partners or competitors but the profitability of firms is considerably weaker for a variety of reasons including the narrowness of the industrial base and the excessive extension of the tertiary sector. When expansion was resumed in the spring of 1968, there were grounds for hope. But policies designed by civil servants taken together with the dreams of General de Gaulle, could well shake the most optimistic— those who would like to believe in the modernization of France.

It seems, according to de Gaulle, that the explosion was in no

139

way connected with government by decree nor with the diminishing importance of parties and assemblies. Nor—according to him—was any part played by civil service authoritarianism, continued and aggravated by ministers who had come into Government from the public service, nor by the excessive pressures exerted on the economy in the hope of ensuring a favourable balance of foreign trade, nor by the way in which the middle-ranking groups were denied any concessions. General de Gaulle clings, like the literary intellectuals, to the metaphysical interpretation, that the cause was the dissatisfactions which people feel in a consumer society. While this interpretation contains a grain of truth, it cannot inspire any effective action. Participation is no more likely to triumph over a loss of reason than was expansion. The young revolutionaries' response to the dream of French greatness was to chant the slogan 'We are all German Jews'—which was allegedly echoed by other demonstrators with a slogan so horrible that I refuse to believe the story.

Neither the young workers nor the young middle class could accept the Gaullist vision of France. On this point I personally feel closer to the Gaullists than to their opponents. I was deeply wounded by this radical negation of patriotism and by the substitution of the name of Che Guevara for that of a resistance hero. But circumstances do explain why they reject the cult of the nation and are indifferent to high politics.

How were the young people able to confuse what went on in the Elysée with what went on in the world? Forty years ago revolutionary negativism found expression to the East of the Rhine, and to a certain extent to the West, in fervent nationalism. Today the real limitations of France are merely underlined by her aping of the Great Powers in such matters as nuclear weapons or the space race. The young people accepted and amplified anti-Americanism, and found a meaning of life in the outlook of the guerilla, in the mob passion of the third world, in pure violence and anarchist Utopia—not in a 'certain idea of France', an idea which belonged to their grandparents. As for the idea of Europe, General de Gaulle has killed it—(perhaps it would never have existed without him?)

I am not one of those who willingly play the Cassandra. I shall not say that the battle is lost before it has been fought, or that the Gaullists are incapable of mastering the consequences of the crisis and the further upheavals which are bound to come. But the reaction of General de Gaulle and his associates to the events was enough to discourage the best intentions: we have had a Prince who sought to change established habits and usages by decree and to force all the French people—save himself—to participate in a dialogue; an intelligentsia divided between hermetic isolation, Maoism and the cult of violence; a Government made up of civil servants, capable of taking and giving orders, but not of practising the art of politics; a Communist Party which has remained internally Stalinist, at odds with revolutionary factions and anxious to retain its position in the unions and in administration; a University torn between the P.S.U. and other revolutionaries, the Communists, and the defenders of the liberal tradition, of whom the last may be the most numerous but the least well organized, and almost disowned by the public authorities; a great mass of students in the Faculties of Letters, and a shortage of engineers and scientists; leftism turning into the conventional outlook both of the victims and the beneficiaries of economic progress. Who would not see from this list, that France is a country which is afraid of modernity, and whose aspirations to the impossible are condemning it to a form of underdevelopment, and whose revolutionary spirit—still verbal, but potentially perhaps effective—has become its spiritual point of honour.

The French people reacted to the events of May in their traditional style; their rejection of sterile strikes and of riots may for a time be enough to hold them together. But where can we look for faith or hope when the Sovereign believed himself to be charged with a mission for which no one else shares responsibility, and whose mystery is not revealed to the eyes of others? Will the personal adventure of one man end in the tragedy of a nation? Let us at least recall the wisdom of the Greeks: 'No one should be called happy until the last day.'

APPENDIX

LE FIGARO

At a time when the written word is as immediate as the spoken, it seems to me that it is a good idea to re-publish some articles of mine which originally appeared in *Le Figaro* during May and June 1968. They are reprinted here as they were with only a few minor alterations, either corrections of fact, or a softening of excessively polemical blows. The articles, written as they were under the immediate impact of the May events, seem to me to form an essential part of this book, which aims to provide a witness's account of his reactions to what happened.

Reflections of an Academic

As an old professor who has loved his profession, it is not without some hesitation and sadness that I comment on the events of the past week. During the days of crisis, I refrained from writing, so as not to contribute to the increasing confusion created by the moves and false moves of one side and another. The Government has piled error on error, but M. Cohn-Bendit, whom the press and radio have turned into something of an historic figure, does not seem to me, for all that, the man to reform the French University.

When student demonstrators suffer brutal police repression, everyone's sympathy naturally goes out to them. (When the demonstrators are from the working class, do the students' parents always react in the same way?)

In a sense and by definition the young cannot be wrong; youth will have the last word and express its feelings about the world and the people in it by its arguments or even more by its actions.

But in Berlin, where I met the angry German students last January, I could not help recalling their militant counterparts of 1930 and 1931 whom I got to know when I myself had only just passed through to the other side of the barricade. They, too, I was told at the time, were necessarily right, since they represented the future (and the future bore the name of Hitler). Even at that time, Professor Marcuse, father of today's young rebels, rejected outright the existing régime—the Weimar Republic. Where will the student revolt end, supposing that it ends anywhere? How have the disconnected, seemingly confined, disturbances of Nanterre grown in the space of a week to the point of shaking the Government and re-establishing in the heart of the University a kind of solidarity—although an illusory if not hypocritical solidarity, which would not last a moment if it came face to face with real problems?

It has been said many times in the press, and there is no doubting this, that the 'liberal' teachers who sought to reform the institutions exerted an overriding influence at Nanterre. In the psychology and sociology departments, the two most restless sections, they had formed staff-student committees on an equal footing (*comités paritaires*) which put into practice the dialogue that was being called for in all quarters. Now the dialogue has degenerated into permanent agitation, occasionally into intolerable grossness, under the direction of the 'German anarchist', as *L'Humanité* has called him.

The day when the widely-respected Dean finally took the decision to suspend classes, many of the teaching staff regretted that his action was so late in coming; no one reproached him for being over-hasty or authoritarian.

Ten days later students and teachers rose up side by side against the authorities. The trade union declared a 24-hour general strike. What had happened in the meantime?

This crazy week started with the police moving into the courtyard of the Sorbonne and the closing of the faculty. On Friday 3rd would the two student groups have come to blows if the police had not intervened? I find it surprising that so many people should be dogmatic on this point when they are either ignorant of the facts or only half-informed.

I have talked to two colleagues who were there on the day; both profess to leftist views, and both are undeniably sincere. But while one assures me that there was no emergency, and that everything would have ended without any drama, the other is equally convinced of the opposite. So I shall not attempt to resolve what is a question of history: not because I fear responsibility, but simply out of ignorance.

This decision—whether mistaken or unavoidable matters little —transformed the situation overnight. The majority of the teachers, traditional or militant, conservative or liberal, experienced a common impulse, and burying their differences, fell in together behind the same banner. Rejuvenated and aroused to indignation, they eagerly joined the ranks of the students (who only the day before had been heckling their lecturers) in denouncing authority. The incidents of almost unbelievable brutality reported by numerous eye-witnesses, the summary arrest and detention of demonstrators or simply passers-by, of students and pseudo-students, did the rest. Episodes of 'Ubu-esque' proportions, like the cake-maker held at gun-point for possessing a knife, made a laughing-stock of the 'guardians of public order'. Passions fed upon themselves. The opposition parties, including the Communists, who were hostile at first, took over the mass movement which thousands of students were joining spontaneously, even though they were being manipulated by others who remained in the background.

Over the Friday night, the rejection of the students' three demands (which Minister rejected them? or was it the President of the Republic himself?) and the action of the police in dispersing the demonstrators entrenched behind the barricades gave rise to some violent, absurd and sometimes tragic clashes.

It took the return of M. Pompidou for the Government finally to muster the courage to capitulate—which is what it should have done four days previously. The students or pseudo-students, arrested or sentenced, have been picked out at random. What purpose lay behind their imprisonment? Whatever your fundamental beliefs, an end had to be made to the Saturnalia that were fast becoming revolution.

The militant groups had succeeded in mobilizing friends, teachers and even the Communist Party. Never since February 1848 had any French Government given such a masterly display of weakness and brutality in turn. As for the demonstrators, they only proved once again that great battles do not need great causes.

Student revolt breaks out in capitalist and socialist countries alike. It breaks out under liberal régimes as well as under dictatorships. From this most commentators conclude that the phenomenon has deep roots—the generation clash, or the nature of the social order, an anonymous and repressive force even in a democracy. Each observer chooses the explanation which best suits his own inclinations: worn-out ideologies; the failure of socialism and capitalism; the mediocrity of the 'consumer society'; poverty in the midst of plenty; black ghettos in the world's most affluent country; the meaninglessness of a university cut off from society, or associated with a society which is devoid of meaning, etc.

Should all the revolts be lumped together—that of the Spanish students deprived of rights enjoyed by the French, of the American students who denounce the Vietnam war, of the Czechs and Poles who aspire to freedoms which in Paris or Berlin are 'questioned' only by the most fervent of those who 'question' the established order? I am well aware of what the students will reply: whether they have freedoms or not their lot remains the same, and so does their 'alienation' or that of the whole society.

Perhaps this is how these young, mainly middle-class, people think or rather feel. And in so far as this is the case, the Government and the professors must look in vain for a way out. These students, ill at ease in the 'University factories', and lost in the lonely crowd, are like the first factory workers of the early nineteenth century who destroyed their machines. The students symbolically smashed tables and chairs, the tools of their work and of their enslavement.

It matters little what truth there is in this interpretation. In each case the teachers, concerned more with their job than with a crusade without a Cross or a struggle without a cause, must set themselves to move patiently and gradually towards the best possible solution of problems which, despite certain common characteristics, take on a particular shape in each country.

15.5.68.

Reflections of an Academic

The Transformation of Higher Education

From Friday 3rd May, while the Government was adding to the confusion, the tide of pseudo-philosophic talk was running high. Professors and students were rebuilding the University, society, life itself. After the 'lyrical illusion' of the days of riot, nothing will ever be the same again, if the real devotees are to be believed. As they see it, the factories which turn out graduates will be in a state of constant change, and not subject to disciplinarian order; sense will drive out non-sense, teachers will have nothing to do but teach, students nothing to do but learn, and both will fulfil their calling in the two-way examination of ideas and the mutual questioning of a consumer society which they despise in theory, but from which in practice they reap benefit.

Let us come back down to earth and make a few elementary observations about the Faculties of Letters, where the crisis raged with the greatest fury. The curriculum reform had been designed for the Faculties of Science, and the Dean, Zamansky, had given it his approval. The variant of the reforms applied to the Faculties of Letters is open to obvious criticism, since it raises barriers between the disciplines at the very time when everyone wants such barriers removed. Furthermore, against the judgment of the deans and the teaching body, the ministry has had the new system applied immediately to students in mid-course, which has led to complications and injustices. The Minister and the Director of Higher Education are aware of the need ultimately to revise the reform and to make decisions which until now have been difficult. (What, for instance, is to become of the *Agrégation* examinations? How should the third cycle be organized? How should the problem of university entrance be tackled?)

Aside from these uncertainties there is the basic question of what to do with the graduates from the arts faculties—and to a lesser extent from the faculties of law and economics. Until recently most graduates went into the teaching profession. There was a kind of vicious circle in which teachers educated students, the best of whom progressed, when the time was ripe, to join the dignified ranks of their mentors.

The build-up of numbers both in the old faculties (such as modern languages) and in the more or less recent schools, (psychology and sociology) has led to a break with tradition. Most of the graduates will not stay on at university, but will take up an active rôle in society where they will have to find a profession.

The *ad hoc* physicians who stand at the bedside of the old, dying University assure us that the students are apprensive about their careers, and that the cause of their unease is their fear of the future. This diagnosis contains an element of truth, but the most revolutionary amongst the students are, it seems to me, less children of the working classes (students who have to earn their living have little leisure to devote to active opposition) than of the bourgeoisie, whose sons and daughters admire the films of J.-L. Godard, dream of Che Guevara, and condemn affluence while driving around in their 2CV's.

One of my colleagues at the Faculty of Science in Lille, M. Savard, addressed his students on these lines: 'You are all, even the poorest amongst you, a privileged group, for you all still have a chance of escaping from the fate of the proletariat, the lot of the worm. Your comrades in the factories no longer have this chance, supposing that they ever had it. Whether the society is capitalist or socialist, it is in large measure at the expense of society that you pursue your studies. The young worker who labours on the building site or toils in the din of the workshop pays taxes so that you may rise above him in the social scale. It is true that your academic merit justifies your privileges. But you would have had a more receptive audience if instead of shouting "We have our rights", you had said: "We are fortunate".'

Overstatements perhaps, but many students from bourgeois backgrounds would nevertheless do well to ponder them.

Student numbers are increasing in all industrial countries; this is a universal trend, and meets certain social needs. But this increase, which will continue over the next few years, inevitably changes the nature of higher education. Either all holders of the baccalauréat are given the right to university entrance, in which case examiners will be obliged to eliminate a number of the students at the end of the first or second year; or else we must adopt the system which operates in most countries, capitalist or socialist, in which the selection process takes place at the completion of secondary education before admission to the University. The first is a so-called democratic formula, and one which I detest. The second comes in for bitter attack by the students' unions and the majority of teachers.

Whichever formula we opt for, there is one simple and fundamental principle which must never be disregarded: a balance
must be maintained between the student numbers and the
available resources—accommodation, staff, libraries, materials.
Now for the past ten years every Minister of National Education
has ignored this principle. They have all both rejected the principle of pre-selection and refused to supply the material and
financial resources which their chosen policy demanded. Some
time or other this absurdity was bound to become clear to
everyone.

The students denounce the technocratic University and selection procedures, and worry about their career prospects at the
same time. Now, in so far as the education the University pro-
vides does not fit students for a profession, how could they have
any guarantee that their degrees will secure them the social
position they aspire to? There has to be either a rigorous process
of selection and a programme designed to bring the numbers of
students and their distribution between faculties into line with
forecast economic demands (difficult to achieve with any accuracy), or freedom of choice with its implicit and explicit risks.
Of course, there remain possible compromises between the two
formulae; but compromise will neither rid us of what some denounce as technocracy, nor remove the apprehension that others
feel about the future.

Once these obvious points have been recalled to mind, can, or
should a dialogue with the students be embarked upon? Indeed
it should. Seen in historical perspective there is more danger
than hope in the present outburst, but the actors in the drama,
with their rejection of conventional watchwords, and their
alienation from old parties, offer, in spite of everything, the
chance of a complete renewal.

16.5.68.

Steadfast and Changing[1]

Times of disorder; derangement of minds; confusion of ideas;
violence of emotions; excessive hopes and excessive fears. A

151

revolution does not lend itself to analysis as it takes place. Anxiety is not conducive to work, but it is allayed in reading the works of those who have lived through similar times, with a clear vision and an unfettered mind. I hope that our readers will be interested, as I am, in one or two excerpts from the 'Souvenirs' which Alexis de Tocqueville wrote concerning the revolution of 1848.

'I have sometimes wondered what could have produced this sudden paralysis of mind in the King. Louis-Philippe had spent his life amidst revolutions, and certainly lacked neither experience nor courage nor intelligence, although these failed him utterly on that day. I believe that his weakness sprang from the greatness of his surprise; he was overwhelmed before he understood what was happening. No one had *foreseen* the February revolution, but it surprised him more than anyone else. No outward sign had prepared him for it, because, several years previously, his mind had withdrawn into that state of haughty solitude which so often overtakes the minds of princes, who, having enjoyed good fortune for so long, mistake luck for genius, and are no longer prepared to listen, thinking that they have nothing more to learn from anyone.'

On the evening of 25th February, 1848, Alexis de Tocqueville met his friend, J.-J.Ampère, son of the renowned physicist, and himself a historian and man of letters teaching at the Collège de France.

'Ampère was a great mind, and what is more important, a man of courage, gentle but firm in his dealings. Unfortunately he was strongly inclined to bring the spirit of the salon into literature, and literature into politics. What I mean by his literary approach to politics was his seeing rather what is clever and novel than what is true; in liking what makes a pretty picture rather than what is serviceable; showing appreciation of the actors' fine performance regardless of the consequences of the play, and, finally, in forming conclusions based less on reason than on impressions. . . .

'What I saw drew me to foresee in the near future some strange disturbances and crises, but at no time did I visualize the plundering of the rich. I understood the people of Paris too well not to know that their first actions in times of revolution are usually generous: that they like to spend the days immediately following their triumph in boasting of their victory, in making show of their authority and in playing the master. . . .

'After February 25th, the impetuous minds of the innovators conceived a thousand bizarre systems which spread among the troubled spirits of the people. It was as though society itself had been reduced to dust from the shock of the revolution, as if it had resorted to open competition to decide the new form of the edifice that was to be raised in its place. Every man put forward his own plan; one in the newspapers, another on the posters which soon covered the walls. Others addressed their fellows in the open air. While one pledged to set right the imbalance of wealth, a second was concerned with the fair distribution of education and knowledge, and a third undertook to eliminate the most ancient of all inequalities—that between man and woman. Plans to fight poverty were proposed, along with remedies for the labour trouble which has been the torment of mankind since its conception. . . .

'I perceived a universal attempt to make the best of the event which fate had just extemporized, and to win over the new master. The men of property liked it to be remembered that they had always been hostile to the middle class, and always favourably disposed to the popular classes. The priests rediscovered the dogma of equality in the Gospel, and insisted that they had always known it was there. The middle class itself recalled somewhat proudly that its forebears had been workers. As much energy was expended in demonstrating all these things as had been spent some time before in their concealment; so true is it that the vanity of men, without changing its nature, can offer the most diverse of spectacles.'

Nobody has ever forgotten the picture that Alexis de Tocqueville painted of the French people at the end of his *L'Ancien Régime et la Révolution*:

'(A people) . . . restive of temperament, and yet adapting more readily to the arbitrary, even violent, rule of a prince than to free and orderly government by its principal citizens; today the avowed enemy of subjugation, tomorrow giving rein to a kind of passion that the nations most inclined to servitude cannot attain. A people that could be led on a string so long as no one resisted, but ungovernable given one instance, somewhere, of rebellion. Thus it always deceives its masters who fear it either too much or too little.'

And lastly these remarks from Renan's *Intellectual and Moral Reform of France:*

'Nowadays—and this is what complicates the task of the reformers—it is the people who must understand. Let us try, with as accurate an analysis as possible, to understand what is wrong with France, so that we may find the appropriate remedy. The patient is exceedingly strong with apparently boundless reserves. His free will is greatly in evidence. It is for the doctor not to make a wrong diagnosis, for a too-rigid treatment or the wrong medicine would revolt the patient, and either kill him or worsen his condition.'

29.5.68.

After the Storm

One hundred and fifty Nanterre students, under the leadership of the 'German anarchist' (Cohn-Bendit), dealt the first blow which precipitated, in a matter of days, the collapse of a rotting edifice—the old University. In two weeks the zeal of youth won over the mass of workers. Ten million strikers paralysed the nation. The rats abandoned the sinking ship of a condemned régime, and the 'vanquished' of May 1958 prepared to pay back in kind the 'victors' of ten years ago, today's legal government. Then suddenly, on Thursday 30th May, a voice was raised which, within a matter of minutes, restored the State and mobilized hundreds of thousands of Parisians, millions of Frenchmen. The fever which had mounted in ten days abated again in the space of a few hours. France emerged from a waking dream, and, in the words of Tocqueville, 'was as surprised as the rest of the world when she saw what she had just done'.

A month ago no-one had foreseen anything. Neither the President of the Republic, nor the Government, nor the members of Parliament, nor the Communist Party, nor the trade unions—nor of course the author of this article. Future historians will tell us that deep causes, 'of an economic nature', made the explosion inevitable. For our contemporaries there are only two logical elements to this mad episode: the detonator and the action of the Communist Party.

Of all France's institutions, the University was the one most seriously afflicted, and there is a part of the student body throughout the world which burns with a revolutionary fire which we find neither in the workers of the U.S.A., who are satisfied with their affluent society, nor in the French workers, who are still officered by the Communist Party. And the Communist Party, during these few weeks when the turmoil threatened at any moment to end in tragedy, did not cease to show its 'statesmanship' to take up the expression of M. Beuve-Méry, editor of *Le Monde* which M. Andrieu remarked on in *L'Humanité*.

At no time did the Communist Party or the CGT call for riot, at no time did they wish to overthrow the Gaullist government whose foreign policy fulfills their every wish and allows them to carry on their gradual infiltration of French society. They would obviously have taken on the task of Government if it had been put into their hands; but their constant objective was not to 'start a revolution', but, at the same time, to avoid being outflanked on their left by the students, the Maoists and the young workers. The mistakes made by the Government are due in part to the excessive confidence it placed in the support of the Communist Party. In the final analysis the Communists did not betray this confidence: in the hour which followed the President of the Republic's speech, the Communist Party defused the bomb, and agreed to elections which it could scarcely hope to win. The C.F.D.T. and the Federation of the Left remain powerless between the two pillars of France—the Communist Party which is biding its time, and the bourgeois State to which most French people rally at times of crisis.

The students, the Geismars and the Sauvageots, the P.S.U. and the intellectuals great and small, ever hankering for a salutary upheaval, are capable of destruction, and over these past weeks have not stinted themselves. Some of their acts of destruction open the way to the future.

But whether they be Proudhoniens or Poujadistes, romantics or cynics, free agents or pawns, whether they be followers of Mao or Castro, the heirs of 1848, or imitators of a China more dreamed of than comprehended, the revolutionaries of May have promoted the cause of one or the other of the two 'parties of order'. The bourgeois party will show them more indulgence than the Communists ever would, once they thought their time had come.

Many of the revolutionaries will accuse the Communist Party of having 'betrayed the revolution'. The Communist Party does not need me to defend it, but I make the plea that by avoiding the maelstrom it acted in its own interests as well as in those of all French people.

The irresponsible are at liberty to prefer the régime of Castro to that of France, and to do their worst to bring the latter down to the level of the former. (Even the revolutionaries of the Sorbonne or of the P.S.U. would be loath to do this.) The Communists know that, if they were to come to power, they would be responsible for an extraordinarily complex and delicate system. The masses would not tolerate the impoverishment that would follow riot in the streets and anarchy in the factories. At the same time the workers want an improved standard of living as well as 'participation'. Before condemning the consumer society one must reap its advantages, however derisory they may appear to the idealists (who are not all prepared to forego them). The French Communists have not given up hope of seeing themselves in power in France at some fairly remote time in the future.

But at the present moment, with most French people against them, and facing the risk of civil war if there were an insurrection, they would have been guilty of 'adventurism' had they heeded the calls of the C.F.D.T. and the intellectuals. M.

Barjonet will fade into obscurity along with several other of the heroes of May.

The relations between the Communist Party and the Gaullist government bear some resemblance to those between the Soviet Union and the United States: a compound of alliance and enmity, of co-operation and competition. The Communist Party, long the enemy of the bourgeois State, still does not fight it, for the moment, in the same indirect way in which the Soviet Union combats the United States in Vietnam. The diplomacy of General de Gaulle, his denunciation of American imperialism and the glorification of the revolutionary movements of the Third World coincide 'objectively' with communist propaganda. In the long term M. Waldeck Rochet is right to prefer Gaullism to the politics of Mendès-France.

Every country has known student revolt, but in France, and in France alone, this revolt grew into a national crisis. One bad speech by President de Gaulle, one ill-timed plebiscite-referendum proposal, and for two days the régime was tottering. Then one fighting speech from an old man of 78, and the people of France rediscovers a sense of reality, petrol pumps and holidays.

We still have to come to understand this episode of French history, the strangest yet in a history rich in strange episodes.

4.6.68.

After the Storm

From Nanterre to the Elysee

Why was France so completely shaken by a student revolt less serious at the onset than similar disturbances at Berkeley and Columbia, in Berlin and Bonn, in Warsaw and Prague? The replies tomorrow's historians make to this question will illustrate the great variety of interpretations that can be put upon events. *Narrative Interpretation:* When the university authorities finally took a strong line, the students of Nanterre descended on the

Sorbonne. The police were called into the courtyard to break up the left-wing demonstrators, who were being threatened by a counter-demonstration outside. Overnight the *enragés* became heroes; 'police at the Sorbonne' became a symbol which both outraged and inspired. The Minister for National Education, who had pledged his reputation, stood up willy-nilly to the demonstrations which grew in number until the first night of the barricades, the night from Friday 10th to Saturday 11th May. The trade unions called a general strike for 24 hours, not so much in support of the students' demands (which were ill-defined) as to appease its ranks with a day of rest and marches— officially to protest against police brutality.

The Prime Minister, who was on a visit to Asia during this first week, saw fit on his return to grant the students what they had demanded in vain on the night when they erected the barricades. But he repudiated, or appeared to repudiate, the action of the police, who took this with some bitterness and became thereafter a source of some anxiety to the Government. After all, many policemen feel closer to the proletariat than to the middle-class students.

The re-opening of the Sorbonne to the students, the capitulation of authority, gave new impetus to the agitation which the Prime Minister was hoping to quell: the President of the Republic, undaunted, left for Rumania where students and workers accorded him the warm reception denied him in France by the forces of occupation in the Sorbonne and the factories. What part was played in the general wave of strikes by the Maoist groups, the young workers and the spontaneous reaction of the masses? No one, I fear, not even the *Renseignements Généraux* (the special intelligence service of the French police) could say with any certainty. When the President returned, France was in the grip of a spreading paralysis. Harassed by the C.D.F.T., the students, the P.S.U. and the intellectuals, the C.G.T. was endeavouring to keep control of its ranks while still negotiating with the Government which it continued to treat as a valid interlocutor.

On Monday 27th the rank and file workers rejected the

Grenelle agreements reached by their leaders. Is this explained by the mood of the masses, the activity of the *groupuscules*, or by a wily ruse of the C.G.T.? On this point again there is uncertainty, but I find it difficult to believe that M. Seguy could willingly have provoked the jeers which greeted his remarks at Javel or Billancourt. At this time the C.F.D.T., still at odds with the C.G.T., was demanding a new government under Mendès-France. On Wednesday 29th May, General de Gaulle left the Élysée. He had not spoken since the previous Friday when the State itself seemed to be tottering on the brink, and the Communist Party was unwillingly calling for a 'popular government'. In Wednesday evening's edition of *Le Monde*, M. Viansson-Ponté announced that the General had retreated *'dans son village et son chagrin'*—'to his village and his grief'. In fact the Head of State was bent on quite another mission: he was making sure that in the event of a general strike turning into insurrection despite the Communist Party, he could rely on the loyalty of his generals.

On Thursday 30th May, the Head of State renounced the referendum and consented to elections—two of the demands made by the opposition—but in such a tone as to make it appear that he had made the decisions of his own sovereign volition. Moreover, since many Frenchmen had taken for granted in the course of the preceding days that either the President of the Republic or the Prime Minister was bound to resign, the continuation in office of the legal government, ratified by hundreds of thousands of Parisians marching down the Champs Elysée, marked an effective victory for the party of order, which spreads far beyond the Gaullist Party, and a defeat for the revolutionaries, if not for the Communist Party. It is a strange country indeed which can be driven to anarchy by one bad speech, but words and character are powerful factors when fate hangs in the balance.

Had General de Gaulle been waiting for the right moment to come before playing his master stroke? Could it be that the speech of the 24th, delivered by a phantom, was intended to highlight the address of the 30th, whose brutally threatening tone and impression of high authority presented the double advantage of allowing the C.G.T. to put its ranks in order and of cutting down to size the revolutionaries of the P.S.U. and U.N.E.F., and thus causing them to lose face? Nobody will ever know, save perhaps a few of the actors in the drama. Was it a wise and well-planned strategy, or was it, as is more likely, a succession of wrong moves which culminated in a temporary, and ill-deserved success?

On the Responsibility of the Institutions: After the riots at Berkeley, in California, the President of the University resigned. Perhaps the President of Columbia in New York will relinquish his post in a few months' time (He has now done so; R.A.). In France the Dean of Nanterre laid the responsibility at the feet of the ministry; the rector of the academy did not call in the police before the minister himself (or his *directeur de cabinet*) had given his approval. In the end the militants of Nanterre involved not only the university authorities, but the Government, the President of the Republic, and the régime itself.

The régime did not originate this essentially misguided administrative centralization, but it has made it worse. What is more it has closed off all the safety valves. It has reduced or suppressed altogether any dialogue with Parliament, the political parties or the unions. France suffers from a weakness of all intermediate institutions, a weakness which is accentuated by the Gaullist method of exercising authority. Who amongst the students had heard of M. Sauveageot before May 1968? Which university considered itself represented by M. Geismar? Fewer than one in four university teachers are members of S.N.E.Sup., and its members have never directed their general secretary to play at revolution. Unfortunately, and in this we are all guilty in as much as we are citizens, we choose, or more often allow to be chosen as managers of our professional organizations, not men distinguished for their work or personality, but specialists in trade-unionism or agitation, politicians in miniature.

Once again the crisis has illuminated the tragically precarious condition of the country's social structures. Even the Communist Party, challenged on its left, has not easily resisted. The façade of order, stability and grandeur was shattered in the course of a few days. The credit that France had acquired abroad has been washed away in the tide of the riots. Once again, the world, with pleasure or regret, had rediscovered the eternal France: a capricious, brilliant, unpredictable nation upon whom no one can rely; one day seemingly apathetic—the next on the barricades, a nation always true to its nature in its sudden voltes-face.

The Psychological Causes: There would have been no eruption, if dissatisfactions and demands had not been allowed to pile up without the Government being fully aware of them. An analysis of the economic predicament could call for a separate study, but there can be no doubt that the nation's leaders, obsessed with their campaign against the dollar, kept the brakes on too long. France's changing society did not inflict hardships on any specific class, but there were victims of inevitable economic growth in several areas and in several categories of workers. It was not the young unemployed who denounced the consumer society.

It remains nonetheless the case that the blaze, even a blaze sparked off by revolutionary *groupuscules*, could not have spread had it not come upon inflammable materials. Flags, red and black, remain the symbols of vague and undefined hopes. Students and workers will have yet one more glowing memory of days of strikes and celebration, of marches, endless discussions and rioting, as if from time to time the sameness of everyday life, the smothering effect of technical and bureaucratic rationalization, required a sudden shake-up, as though the French only came out of their shell in a revolutionary psychodrama. Participation is a vague word but a powerful concept, which expresses an aspiration to the kind of community life which our hierarchical, neatly partitioned-off society with its juxtaposition of privileges, only offers to the people in the brief moments of the 'romantic illusion'.

Has the earth tremor on this occasion shaken the structures to the point of making possible, not the replacement of one mob of politicians by another, but the introduction of reforms, prosaic

to be sure, but more genuine than those dreamt of by intellectuals in their delirium or by the Communists as they lie in wait?
5.6.68.

Remarks for Adults

A friend asked me, after the appearance of the *Le Figaro* article of 29th May, how Alexis de Tocqueville responded to the enthusiasm of J.-J. Ampère on the evening of the 25th February 1848. After some considerable hesitation, I decided against reproducing these remarks at the time, as they were so pessimistic. Two weeks ago the 'revolutionaries' started putting into practice their favourite slogan: 'No freedom for freedom's foes'; events give us some respite, and I should like now to recall the text in which de Tocqueville expresses the feelings of 'outrage, sorrow and anger' which were boiling in him. 'You understand nothing of what is happening; you look at it like a Parisian stroller or a poet. You call it the triumph of freedom—it is its crowning defeat. I tell you that this people, which you so naïvely admire, has just demonstrated that it is both incapable and unworthy of living in freedom. Show me what experience has taught it. What new virtues has it acquired? Of what old vices has it been delivered? No, say I; it is still the same; just as impatient, just as unthinking, just as contemptuous of the law, just as weak before example and reckless in the face of danger as were its fathers before it. Time has wrought no change in it, but left it as wanton now in serious matters as it once was in trifles.'

And Tocqueville concluded: 'After a deal of shouting we ended by both calling to the future—an enlightened and upright judge, but one, alas, who always arrives too late.'

Since the beginning of May I have had similar dialogues with numerous friends. To what, I asked, could the overthrow of the Gaullist Government by the student–worker riots lead? A government of the left, presided over by M. Mitterand or M. Mendès-France, with or without communist participation, would soon have to lean on one or the other of the two real forces—either on the Communist Party on the one hand which, despite the Castroite, Maoist or P.S.U. troublemakers, represents a possible order, or on the anti-communist majority which normally asserts itself at elections? Part of this majority votes for the moderate left. Perhaps even that part of the anti-communist electorate which is hostile to conservatism or to Gaullism would, in a few months or years, have allowed the election of a president of the left who would not yet be the pawn of the Communist Party.

The May revolution has, for the moment, dispelled these hopes. Either elections will give a majority to the parties of the left, and in this case the Communist Party will exercise the reality of power—albeit via the medium of Mitterand; or, and this is the view to which observers today are more inclined, the fear inspired by the riots will throw the majority of France back onto Gaullism, including those who condemn it and reproach it for its style of condescending authority, its growing tendency to create areas of society reserved to its devotees, its rejection of a genuine dialogue with the citizens and their representatives, and its loss of contact with the real life of France. In other words, the result of the crisis will be a country split in two; either a communist-dominated left, or a Gaullism which may become both more rigid and weaker as a result of the memory of the days of panic.

The *New York Times* wrote a few days ago that General de Gaulle was once again offering the country a choice between himself and chaos, but that France had no real choice since it was favoured simultaneously both with the presence of de Gaulle at the top and with chaos at the bottom. Will this formula, strictly accurate at the given moment, convince the electors that they must first eliminate de Gaulle, or that the first thing to do is to emerge from chaos?

A Gaullist victory at the elections, however overwhelming, would solve nothing in itself. Let us make the most optimistic hypotheses. Let us assume that General de Gaulle and M. Pompidou have the intelligence to 'rise above their victory'; and

that far from retaining their monopoly of power with its atten-
dant advantages, they are prepared to try to broaden the parliamentary base of the Government and to transform the Union
for the Defence of the Fifth Republic into a large party which is
alive and modern, instead of freezing it in a state of unconditional support (which, as events have proved, does not even
offer a guarantee of loyalty).

Even if this optimistic hypothesis were to become reality, this
would not prevent the continued existence of the two causes
which ensure the continuation of the crisis. The minority left—
workers, young people, the Communist Party and the unions—
will feel themselves to be more excluded and alienated than
ever before. The left's feeling of betrayal will be increased by
the fact that during May it challenged the democratic principle
of legality (elections), and that it will find itself faced with a
government whose ways it detests and whose electors—the
defenders of order, the bourgeoisie—it despises.

To this psycho-social tension must be added the material consequences of the weeks of paralysis and riot. The experts still
hesitate to count the cost to the national budget and to industry
of wage increases granted to civil servants, to public service
employees and to workers—and the cost to the entire country of
the weeks of strikes and lost exports. Even if this cost proves in
the end to be lower than is feared today, small businesses will
experience increased difficulties and will disappear more rapidly.
Prosperous firms will attempt to cope with competition by making extra efforts towards rationalization, which will result in
increased unemployment, particularly amongst the young.

In the hall of the *Institut d'études politiques*, hung for the first
time in red curtains, a student to whom I was outlining these
possibilities, replied, in a tone which he intended to be fierce:
'So much the better. The worse the situation becomes, the
greater chance we shall have of destroying society.'

I am not unaware of the significance and the extent of the
feelings of hate which some young people—who perhaps are
more noisy than numerous—hold or affect towards the established order. But the capitulation of the adult population, which

is trying to match the infantilism of its children, is far more striking even than this hatred.

And so it is to the adults I address myself—though I see hardly any (unless their childishness is a mask for cynicism) either in the P.S.U. or the U.N.E.F. or in S.N.E.-Sup. The political problems that have been raised (we shall deal with the problems of the University and the consumer society on another occasion) are, unfortunately, the result of the combined faults of the Gaullist Government and the moderate left; in simple terms: the important thing is first to restore the sense of democratic legality, that is to say in our times, of electoral legality, the only defence against civil war and totalitarianism. This restoration depends first and foremost on the electors themselves. If the results of the elections permit this restoration it will then be for the Gaullists to learn from the lesson.

Gaullism, in the form it took up to May 1968, is over. It has fallen victim to the 'shipwreck of age', and to its own self-contradiction: too liberal for its authoritarian elements, too authoritarian for any liberalism. Victory tomorrow might give it an illusion of power, but if it gave way to this illusion, then Tocqueville's dark prophecies from the evening of February 25th 1848 would become tragic reality; Gaullism must either consent to change, or lose whatever liberalism it had, and by becoming even more inflexible, it will set the stage for a confrontation that is already foreshadowed but is not yet inevitable.

10.6.68.

The University Crisis

The workers have nearly all returned to work. The secondary-school teachers are still on strike. The faculty premises and those of many other higher education institutions remain occupied. The leaders of certain teachers' unions refuse to enter into any dialogue with the legal Government and are carrying on a revolutionary campaign not in their own name but in that of the unions which they no longer represent and the professorial body that they represent even less.

Neither public nor Government opinion has yet appreciated the gravity of the crisis. Youth is restless in every country in the world, but in France the student revolt, by force of diverse circumstances, has assumed a unique character. The students of Prague or Warsaw are rebelling for freedoms already enjoyed by their French counterparts. The latter formulate a number of legitimate demands based on genuine grievances, but a small minority amongst them, thanks to the capitulation of many of the teachers, and to the political innocence of the mass of students and traditionalist professors, are in the process of accomplishing a truly subversive operation which ministers, parents, teachers and students alike refuse to understand; they want to drive the Government of the University and of the State to make a choice between the alternatives of 'student power' terrorism, or of the closure, pure and simple, for an indefinite period, of the faculties of arts (the situation seems less serious in the other faculties).

My readers should not be surprised by the personal and anguished tone of the four articles which follow. In the present situation an effort to understand does not preclude an urge to act.

11.6.68.

The University Crisis

In the Name of the Silent

In a special supplement of *L'Express* entitled 'The Confrontation' (*L'Affrontement*), a certain M. Gerard Bonnot wrote the following: 'M. Raymond Aron, the overlord of the Sorbonne's sociology students, is silent. Last Wednesday he suggested that the readers of *Le Figaro* re-read Tocqueville (1805–59).' And after a few lines devoted to M. Louis Althusser and to M. Michel Foucault, he concluded: 'Of all the avowed "thinkers" only one has been to confront the students on their own ground —Jean Paul Sartre.'

166

M. Gerard Bonnot is unaware that last January I voluntarily gave up the Chair of Sociology which I held at the Sorbonne, both because I was disheartened by the present organization of the University, and because I prefer solitude and work to the 'mandarinate' which, if one is to believe what one reads in the papers, constitutes the teachers' sole ambition.

For ten years I have been a constant critic of the existing structure of our University. I was one of the reformers, and was seen as a dangerous innovator by certain of the teachers, some of whom then discovered in May 1968 that they had a vocation to revolution. A few years ago a Minister in the Civil Service informed me with a smile that I was the *bête noire* of the Society of *Agrégés*. My articles published in this paper in 1960, in which I criticized our examination and *concours* system, in particular the *agrégation*, brought me some malicious replies, including some insulting anonymous letters. Having neither defended nor justified the University of yesterday which no longer exists, I will not accept that today everybody, ministers, parents and journalists should lay their guilt on the heads of the teachers.

From the top of the ladder to the bottom, from the President of the Republic to the last journalist of *Le Monde* or *L'Express*, any one of them can say that 'the University was unable to reform itself'. Indeed, but need I remind the President of the Republic that on three occasions in the last few years he convened an interministerial committee to deal with university problems and that he issued *precise instructions which had not the slightest effect*.

As to the abuse of examinations, I detest the French obsession with them, and I detested it before May 1968; but a society which wants itself to be democratic condemns its youth to competition. It is no different in the Socialist countries. English or American students do not experience the anguish of examinations to the same degree, but this is because the teaching staff have never been asked to eliminate a third or a half of all university entrants after one or two years of university studies. The minister knew full well that by rejecting selection at the university entrance stage he was putting the professors in a position where they had to make this selection, like it or not. It would be a singular demonstration of bad faith to reproach them today with having carried out a function which was tacitly but unmistakably entrusted to them. (Although they might have been able to do it better.)

I should like to illustrate these remarks with an anecdote which I guarantee is authentic. At the time of the Fouchet-Aigrain reform, I had proposed that in the fourth year, when students were proceeding to their master's degree (the *Maitrise*), that one single test should be held: that the student should compose an essay which he would then discuss with his teacher. At the Hotel Matignon they decided that an examination reduced to one single test would be lacking in seriousness, and they called for an additional test—a 'test of knowledge', i.e. the most unreliable of tests. No candidate ever possesses complete knowledge and such a test risks falling to the level of a television quiz.

In 1967, when the arts faculties began their new year, they were keenly affected, particularly in Paris, by the immediate and total imposition of the new system. The teaching body were almost unanimous in warning the ministry, but the latter took no heed and created by its sovereign decision a degree of chaos which was both foreseeable and foreseen.

I am not pleading the teachers' cause against the ministers, but I deny the ministers the right to put the teachers in the dock. In the University of the past the teachers had no power to organize the curriculum, to choose their students or to maintain a reasonable balance between the student numbers and the facilities available (premises, funds, staffing).

The assembly of the Sorbonne and the departmental assemblies had virtually no control over anything. When there is no management, what is the point of co-management? At the Centre of Sociology in the Sorbonne, from 1966–67 onwards I had an annual fund of 10,000 francs: what is the good of a joint-committee with equal representation to distribute a pittance like that?

And what of the responsibility of the teachers during the

crisis? The great decisions of the first week: the closing of Nanterre, the entry of the police into the Sorbonne courtyard; the
refusal to give in to the students' demands on the night of the
10th, M. Pompidou's capitulation on his return, the re-opening
of the Sorbonne to the students, or to all who so call themselves
—these decisions were taken either by the ministers or by agreement with them. It is too late or too early to pass judgment on
any one of them. The responsibility of M. Joxe on the night of
Friday 10th, and that of M. Pompidou on the night of Saturday
11th will provide historians with a theme for endless discussion.

As for the parents who are worried today by the threat of subversion, at the beginning of May these same parents were admir-
ing the exploits of their children as they grappled with the police.
The teachers, or at least those whose voices were heard at that
time, took the side of the students, even of the extremists, the
enragés. True, but how many of those who hold it against them
today were of a similar mind a month ago?

If I am not proud today to belong to the University—too
many personal scores being settled, too much ideological raving,
too much demagogy, too much careerism ('move out of there
so I can take your place') too much 'poujadism' which, under a
pretext of egalitarianism, expresses only a rejection of the higher
values, including talent and learning—I would admire any
minister, any journalist, any writer or trade-unionist who is
genuinely proud of the category to which *he* belongs. (Here, of
course, I exclude the anarchists or nihilists, aesthetes of destruction, and the ex-Communists who believe they are reliving 'the
universal rule of the Soviets'.)

I am not unaware that there is a sincere desire in many
French people to 'change the world'. The revolution goes on,
and no one knows which of its children will be devoured. But
today in the University, as in the Republic, there is one impera-
tive, and only one; we must make an end of this revolutionary
masquerade with its action committees, its plenary assemblies
and general assemblies, these grotesque caricatures of the
Jacobin Commune; in a word there must be a return to law;
not in order to resuscitate a dead University, but to allow us at

169

if it would not be fitting to elect a member of the Scientific Council to the Committee. Whereupon someone in the assembly asked, amidst laughter: 'What is the Scientific Council and who is in it?' The president read out the names of the five members of the Council. With one voice the assembly rejected the proposal. A well-known technique for humiliating the 'mandarins'.

The president had declared in advance that he himself was sufficiently representative of the ex-professoriat, which was evidence of some humour, conscious or unconscious.

Then a fairly confused discussion got under way bearing upon the status of this plenary assembly, upon the relationship between the general assembly of one section of the Institution, and the general assembly[3] of all the sections. The former teachers who belong neither to S.N.E.-Sup. nor to the leftist group, deep down detest this tomfoolery. A plenary assembly is intended to be, and can be nothing other than 'revolutionary'. It does not and cannot have any legality. But the *bona fide* teachers, partisans of reform, are inevitably divided over what tactics to adopt. Should they join in the 'revolutionary game' so as to get the movement flowing along a clear line and seize the chance for the reforms they desire? Or should they immediately voice a categoric 'no'? Initially there was room for doubt and I do not set myself up as a judge over what happened then. But today the answer must be '*no*'.

The assembly voted on a series of motions which tended to create a '*de facto* revolutionary legality', then, after I had left the room, elected a reform commission of thirty members (fifteen for the higher graded teachers, fifteen for the other teaching categories and administrative personnel.)

Outside I chatted for a few minutes with some colleagues who looked indulgently upon these childish goings-on which lead nowhere.

I fear they may be wrong to do so. They are familiar neither with the Communist technique of manipulation, nor the technique, now re-christened Maoist, of direct democracy—the technique, in fact, of terrorism. To take part in discussion at assemblies like this implies the recognition of a pseudo-institution which, for me, does not exist. I repudiate the claims of these assemblies, whether they call themselves plenary or general, to have any authority or to speak for anyone but themselves, and I appeal to the Minister for National Education, before it is too late, to refute the plenary assemblies, and ask that while taking note of all the projects drawn up by the reform commissions, just as with all projects drawn up by private parties, he should not consider these assemblies or the commissions to be representative of any persons other than themselves.

The time is near when compromise will slide into surrender of principle.

A number of my colleagues who also wish to save the faculties are afraid that, by adopting an intransigent attitude, they will open the way to the militants, and produce an irreparable rupture in the collegiate unity of teachers and the even more precarious unity of teachers and students. I respect their view but I cannot accept it. Either the 'manipulators' will win the day— if for instance, the legal Government, either through demagogy or cowardice, were to attempt to appease the students by sacrificing teachers and teaching. In such a case the teachers who refuse to be subjected to a Chinese-type tyranny will have no choice but to resign. Or else, after the elections, teachers, students and ministers will endeavour to build a new University, but not the terrorist University where militants would rule. In this eventuality contact with youth might be re-established by those who today are the object of a general hostility ('they are not playing the game'), but who will at least have salvaged their self-respect.

13.6.68.

The University Crisis—3

Against the Institution of Terrorism

No-one knows the total extent of the work carried out by the reform commissions in the various faculties in Paris and the provinces. I have no doubt that the students and teachers have come to know one another better after this marathon of words—the longest in the history of France, I think, but not the richest in new ideas.

What has risen to the surface again is the old basis of French socialism, a mixture of Proudhonism and Poujadism which had lain hidden under the Marxist-Leninism imported from Russia. The fervour of youth fed on the myths of Cuba and Mao has caused an upset to communist discipline; the latent anarchism of the French has shown to a dazed world how an obsolescent revolution taking models from the nation's unconscious, and a technique of subversion tried and tested outside, can, in the space of a few weeks, precipitate the collapse of a society in the process of modernization, a society opposed both by the victims and the beneficiaries of material progress.

Yet here again I would plead in the name of those who are silent. The overwhelming majority of students must not be confused with the militants. Many have worked seriously and sincerely for the establishment of new structures.

I have been told by my friends that in the faculties of medicine, science, law and economics, and even in certain departments of the arts faculties, the projects which have been worked out will be a guide to the legislators of the future. Some ideas which had already got some footing before the crisis have now to a certain degree been taken up everywhere: organization of the department (or section) the autonomy of the faculties (or universities?), co-management.

While I do not reject the co-management idea in principle no answer has yet been given to the problems which its application would provide. The French University has no resources of its own; will the state, then, or ultimately the tax-payer, provide funds without guarantee or control to university bodies working on the self-management principle? How much money? To cater for how many students? Will the state entrust the management of the universities, faculties or departments to these so-called equal-representation bodies comprising teachers, administrators and students? Are the revolutionaries counting on the bourgeois state to finance a University run on Cuban lines? In the sciences, in medicine, and perhaps in law *contestation* cannot go beyond certain bounds, and the students or researchers who want to improve their technical qualifications may get the better of their comrades who are impatient for social revolution or an accelerated career.

In philosophy and sociology there is no limit to the contestation which is possible, and the extremists usually have the last word. Need one recall this prime truth: the rules of scientific research or teaching have nothing in common with the techniques of political discussion, (newly re-named *contestation*).

Let us, despite everything, place our trust in youth. Let us suppose that the combined student-teacher committees (to which would be added the representatives of the administrative personnel) are made up of men who want to work together and not to bring work to a standstill. Let us suppose that the harm done is no more than time wasted and pointless talk.

This optimistic hypothesis depends on certain strict conditions being met:

1. *It is unthinkable that the students should in any way participate in the election of teachers.*

2. *It is unthinkable that the students should in any way fulfil the function of examiners.*

3. *It is unthinkable that those who represent teachers in the combined teacher-student committees should be elected by general assemblies which include students and delegates of the administrative staff.*

Some of the projects emanating from the Sorbonne and from some other arts faculties, reflect not a drive for reforms but a desire to destroy. When the manipulators of these committees, or assemblies, are not trying to play one group off against another, they do not conceal, even from themselves, that their goal is to overturn first the University and then society.

M. Jean-Jacques Mayoux, whose opinions are far removed from mine, finally understood what was at issue: the 'democratization' which the manipulators are aiming for is seen by some as the same thing as 'student power', that is to say the

Cuban model or what they believe to be the Maoist model, and by others as the strengthening of communist control via the disintegration of the old organizations.

The only chance of salvaging anything of the liberal tradition, of the intellectual and moral values for which the University remains accountable before history, is to reject any deal on the three simple and fundamental principles I have just quoted. This would not be worth mentioning if the French intelligentsia were not living through a crisis of frenzy which is Utopian at one moment and nihilistic the next.

While the self-governing units are still undefined in their organization and resources, the teacher-student relationship is still a subject of vague speculation; thousands of French people seem to have been infected with the fever of self-criticism— another imitation of the Chinese cultural revolution. In this respect the step taken by the journalists of O.R.T.F. in going to plead their cause before the crowds of the Commune deserves to go down in history. As an ardent television fan of rugby, I still wonder for what sins the admirable Roger Couderc was supposed to atone.

So now the revolutionaries have discovered a new source of alienation—knowledge. The teacher who declares himself to be a man of knowledge superior to that of his students allegedly laid claim to an authority which the young people found intolerable. This may be true. But my memory of my young days is very different. I looked for men to admire, living men if I could find them, dead men if I could not. If, for motives that might be revealed by psycho-analysis, the young hate both their father and their master, they will hate even more a father who capitulates and a master who humiliates himself. We must ensure that these young people who want to fight and to destroy at least find themselves faced with adults who stand erect instead of on their knees.

In other circumstances I should certainly be as inclined to philosophic analysis as my colleague Ricoeur. I too would say, because in a sense it is true, that the teacher learns from his contact with the students (when he can establish contact). Yes, all teaching should be directed towards a dialogue and an exchange of ideas. Yes, knowledge can easily become crystallized into dogmatism—and this means violence and despotism. But let us get back to earth and ask what is it all about?

In the first and second years of the Arts Faculties the professor finds himself facing several hundred students. He has to choose between two courses: he can either lecture (the *cours magistral*), or he can invite his students to attend seminars. The constantly repeated attacks on the first of these alternatives in the end becomes absurd and ridiculous; first because of the increased number of hours of practical and supervised work, and then because the *cours magistraux* are often of greater value than all the talk expended on *contestation*.

I do not deny the vital importance of the teacher-student relationship. The traditional methods are ill-suited to the teaching of an enormous crowd of students. But what methods *are* suitable for the education of a student body of these proportions? The reforms envisaged by the commissions seem to have one feature in common—they assume, first and foremost, the recruitment of a greater number of staff for the same number of students. Who will enter the faculty? How will selection operate? What career prospects can be offered to graduates? In the midst of this deluge of empty words and vague ideas no-one is concerned with the essential problem.

The rebellion of certain young people against the professors and all the disciplines goes a long way beyond the confines of the University; when a student tells me that he loathes everything his father stands for, what can I do? In the sciences and in research institutes, the generation clash can become extremely intense because the young of 25 to 30 sometimes know more than their 'bosses'. Even in the human sciences the young know how to employ techniques which are unfamiliar to their elders. I willingly admit to my own short-comings. But the revolt of the first-year students of sociology, philosophy or psychology, has nothing to do with the superior knowledge of young scientists or the demotion of old scientists because they cannot keep up with the speed with which new information piles up.

The revolt of the *enragés*, as we have seen, has no tangible objective, and no ideology, was abetted by the complacency of the university authorities and the Government, and must lead either to institutionalized terrorism or to a long lasting close-down of the arts faculties unless the majority both of students and teachers finally find strength and courage enough to defeat both the cowardly and the violent.

14.6.68.

The Fate of the University Depends on the Students

Last week I asked why it was in France, and only in France, that a student revolt had led to a national crisis. Similarly we must ask ourselves why it was that the Nanterre revolt gradually spread to every faculty, every university, every institution of higher education almost without exception. Why is the Government apparently in danger of being as powerless after the elections as it is today?

One immediate answer to this question comes almost automatically to the pen: everything that the historians of the Great Revolution tried in vain to explain—the contagion of revolution, the dissolution of social bonds, the great fear, the stirring-up of basic passions, the return to the state of nature—has become part of our experience—we have seen it, we have lived through it and we have understood it in so far as the most primitive form of crowd psychology as set out for instance by Gustave Le Bon or Pareto allows us to speak of understanding anything.

Of course, more enlightened or more indulgent observers will look for and find other causes. They will claim that the French University was in a more advanced state of sclerosis, more anachronistic, than any other. But it is equally true that despite all its faults, the French University has made enormous progress compared with the Italian University. If a general formula must be stated, it would have to say that the national crisis and the university crisis both stem from the same mixture of libertarian revolt with modernity. Journalists tell us in one breath of students whose diplomas do not guarantee them any career prospects, and in the next of students at the *Institut d'études politiques* who bellow their hatred of the consumer society as they drive around in the cars their parents have given them.

Within the University this highly-charged mixture has acquired an extraordinarily explosive force. Nowhere else was there such a marked contrast between the activism of revolutionary minorities and the passivity of the great majority of students and teachers. Nowhere were the forces of order seen to be so weak. Nowhere has the emotionalism of the left, despite its lack of defined targets and despite its unawareness of the way society works, paralysed resistance to such an extent. Nowhere has an ignorance of politics showed itself in so much purity (or puerility). Nowhere did personal values degenerate with such ease into an abdication of civic responsibility. Nowhere did the *groupuscules* have such an opportunity to put their fanaticism and their techniques to use, and to exploit their talent for destruction.

The governments of the Fourth and Fifth Republics showed just as much blindness as the governments of the nineteenth century in the way in which they crammed 130,000 students, the bourgeois equivalent of the nineteenth-century workers' masses, into the capital. Fewer than 10 per cent of these students belonged to any union. In all probability, fewer than 10 per cent had the slightest thought in April of any university or social revolution. But the typical pattern of provocation-repression, repression-revolt, revolt-repression, which was started off by the blunders of the Government, or which may have been deliberately sought by the ringleaders of the revolt, served to mobilize public opinion and the university teachers in support of the students. This lasted until the moment when the students' parents began to realize that their children's exploits, carried much further by industrial strikes, were beginning to endanger themselves, their interests and the society in which they lived.

Most workers have returned to their jobs, at least for the moment. The students are still talking. They do not have to earn their living by working (I mean by educating themselves).

What do they want now? Everything and nothing. Probably the majority would like to take their examinations, acquire an education, and find a job. For the moment they also want to take part in the reform of the University—good for them! and to change the world—and why not? But in the present climate, many students—even moderates—get carried away when they form themselves into a group. They have overthrown the Bastille of the University for lack of the greater prize of the Élysée. They have become Persons of Some Importance (in Alain's sense of the word), even before they have attained the age of reason. How could they fail to be proud of their victory when so many teachers in *lycées* and universities alike have launched into self-criticism, and when those very professors who only a short time ago rejected the idea of sitting in the same assembly as *maîtres-assistants* and *assistants* have now shown themselves willing to accept the sovereign decisions of the general assemblies where children and old men sit side by side, and where voting by a show of hands is a symbol of the abdication of democracy to the will of the crowd?

It was the population bulge of people born between 1945 and 1950, in the immediate post-war period, which made the 1968 Revolution in the University possible, and in part at least in the country at large. It was as though French institutions, some too inflexible and hide-bound by history, and others too weak, with their mortar not yet set, were blown up by the combination of a slow-down in economic growth and a heavy concentration of students in the University, underscored by the post-war generation pouring into the lecture theatres and on to the labour market.

In spite of everything I have not yet lost all hope that a new University, more vital and better adapted to the demands made on it, may arise from the confusion. I admit there are grounds for viewing the future restoration with some apprehension, but in the immediate future the thing to be feared most in the arts faculties is either the total abdication of responsibility by the adult members with the joint triumph of obscurantism and terrorism, or chaos pure and simple.

I would ask parents and colleagues who are angered by these articles, to consider the case with me. The voluntary discipline of the students is the basis and pre-condition for the very existence of the University. Professors and university authorities have no way of maintaining order if a handful of students is bent on causing disruption. It is true that you cannot force workers to keep up production by threatening them with tanks, but then workers have to work in order to live. This is not the case with students. I am in favour of students being given an increased say in the organization of studies, and a greater share in the management of departments and faculties, although the French have never shown any marked talent for rule by committee. But all these reforms will be meaningful only when the students reject as their representatives those who have been calling the odds over the last few weeks.

During the one and only year when I was responsible for the (unofficial) sociology department, I organized regular meetings with the *assistants* and with student representatives (from the U.N.E.F. and the study groups). I made it clear to the students from the start that I would do my best to solve problems by consultation with them, but subject to the condition that they would behave like 'managers' with a concern for efficiency, and that political action of whatever kind would be indulged in only outside this function. A one-day strike led some of them to start heckling: that was the end of my experiment in forming committees in which students and teachers participated on an equal footing.

The reforms put forward in the teacher-student relationship pre-suppose that the students will acquire a sense of their own responsibilities, and will maintain discipline among themselves.

Has any thought been given over these weeks to the most pressing problem, which in the arts faculties especially assumes dramatic proportions? Most of those who passed the *baccalauréat* in 1968 will go to university in October. The bottleneck in Paris will make it almost physically impossible to re-open the Sorbonne and Nanterre. The newspapers committed to the cult of youth and of the old left will keep on babbling demagogy about

181

the critical university and other intellectual deliria on pain of losing their popularity. There will perhaps be a 'critical university' in which young French men will discuss Mao's little red book, the writings of Che Guevara and the esoteric prose of the 'in' magazines; but there will be no University at all if by University we understand a community to which those who lack knowledge come to learn something from those who are a little less ignorant.

The *enragés* certainly know more than their teachers about barricades and revolutionary warfare. If this henceforth is to be the object of the 'critical university', then there is no longer any room for professors at the Sorbonne unless they are prepared to worship the great God Marx and all his prophets.

It remains to be seen whether the bourgeois State will maintain a school for revolutionaries, and what careers other than that of the guerilla will be open to students brought up on a diet of undiluted *contestation*.

15/16.6.68.

The University Crisis

Conclusions and Propositions

We all lived through these weeks of confusion on our emotions. No-one was able to keep a cool head and clear vision throughout.

Some people were sympathetic with the elements of revolt, generosity and hope which they saw in the youth movement. Others have been struck by the way in which adults—the university authorities and the Government—abdicated responsibility. Others again saw this enormous upheaval as an opportunity to transform the structure of the universities, a structure so anachronistic that only the blind could fail to see it. The leaders of some students' and teachers' unions exploited the situation and conducted a genuinely subversive campaign. Some academics applauded the political exploits of the U.N.E.F. and the S.N.E.-Sup.; others were angered by them.

There were some episodes which pained us to the very core

of our being. Two lecture rooms, one in Strasbourg, one in the Sorbonne, had been named after Jean Cavaillès, a professor of the philosophy of science, who had been shot by the Nazis as the head of a Resistance group. The students tore down the plaques which bore his name, a name which symbolized everything that is best in us. Perhaps they did not know what they were doing; perhaps they wanted to debunk the idea of patriotism. Mutual lack of understanding took on tragic proportions; our very reasons for living were now at stake.

Let us try once more to find peace, peace both in the country and peace in our minds.

What is the reply I received from hundreds of teachers, students and parents who have written to me? We must get away from chaos, from anarchy, from violence. The University cannot be reformed throughout in a few weeks on the basis of *ad hoc* measures or by decisions made in so-called plenary or general assemblies. So I shall sum up, if I may, the main points of my preceding four articles.

1. The students' revolt did not start spontaneously with the aim of reforming the University. It was triggered off by the 'March 22nd Movement' and other *groupuscules* who never claimed to be concerned with the reform of studies or of student-teacher relationships. In the first week the students showed their solidarity with the *enragés* against the police and the Government. Up to and after 30th May the leaders of the U.N.E.F., and with some reluctance those of the S.N.E.-Sup. pursued a genuinely revolutionary course which had as its aim the overthrow of the Government by insurrection. The members of the S.N.E.-Sup. have a perfect right to approve of their leaders' revolutionary action, but they cannot fail to be aware of the reactions of those of their colleagues who are anxious for the fate of the University, hostile to subversion, and hostile to the rôle played by a union which claims to be representative while having only 20 per cent of teachers in institutes of higher education among its members.

2. After the occupation of the Sorbonne, followed gradually by the occupation of almost all university premises, the students

managed to find time, between two all-night riots and attempts to visit strikers in their factories, to set up commissions to study the reform of the University. In collaboration with some teachers, their plenary or general assemblies adopted resolutions and sometimes envisaged the re-organization of departments (or sections), faculties or universities. I totally deny these assemblies any legal validity, even if they used a secret ballot, and even if there were any question of a behind-the-scenes deal between the former masters and the new ones. The Prime Minister and the Minister of National Education have satisfied this demand; nothing which was done in the course of these weeks has any legal validity.

3. I in no way condemn those *assistants, maîtres-assistants* and professors who sought, sometimes with considerable courage, to maintain contact with the students by participating in the work of the commissions and in the plenary and general assemblies. Personally I think the time has now come to end action of this kind. But nothing is further from my mind than to discriminate between those who took part and those who refused to do so as between goats and sheep, between bad and good. There were 'bad' and 'good' in both categories. Let us not indulge in the settling of old scores.

4. No judgments can be made on the work carried out by the commissions nor on the reform plans which were drawn up; no one yet knows the total extent of this work. I have no doubt that the Government will be in a position to retain several proposals drafted by the commissions in some institutions and in some departments. And care must be taken to see that these proposals which may be acceptable in themselves are not deflected from their purpose and exploited by activist minorities in the furtherance of their own causes, which do not include the good of the University.

5. A degree of unanimity has been achieved about some ideas which are valid but, unfortunately, not clearly defined. These include a rapprochement between teachers and students, and increased participation by students in the organization of studies and the management of departments, faculties and universities.

The very people who support these ideas fully and without reservation—these people above all—must bear in mind the conditions under which these ideas can be executed:

(*a*) In all cases *the only acceptable voting method is by secret ballot, with a quorum of participation.* All decisions taken by a show of hands are null and void.

(*b*) *In no circumstances should co-operation between staff and students be allowed to call the dignity and responsibility of teachers into question.* Any election of professors (or the representatives of professors) by an assembly which includes student members is incompatible with that dignity and responsibility.

(*c*) *The degree of student participation in management, which as far as teaching and syllabus are concerned must be kept within certain defined limits, must vary according to the size of the unit concerned* (a department of a few dozen students or a faculty of thousands), *to the educational level of the students, and to the particular discipline being studied.*

(*d*) *The University must unconditionally oppose the degree of political involvement which lies behind slogans like 'permanent contestation' or 'critical university'.* A rational consideration of political problems is a very different thing from public meetings and inter-party debates. Anywhere in the world these slogans lead to riot.

6. Since their reconstitution under the Third Republic, the universities have been subject to the suffocating overlordship of the Ministry of National Education. Now they are making legitimate demands for 'autonomy'. But the universities still receive their financial resources from the State or from the regions, and ultimately from the taxpayers. Are the equal-representation committees the best method of management for organizations which are sometimes a great deal too large, and in which the same rules of efficiency as in industry apply? Moreover, unless the teachers give up their civil service status, unless the administrative structure, based on qualifications and seniority, is abolished in another 'night of 4th August', unless national examinations (such as C.A.P.E.S. and the *agrégation*) are done away with, autonomy will inevitably always be limited. At all events, autonomy can never mean the same things for depart-

185

ments, for faculties and for universities, nor for a faculty of 300 students compared with a faculty of 30,000.

7. The University has a right, indeed a duty, in the interests of the nation and not exclusively in its own interest, to keep up impartial research, and to pass on and to develop fields of learning which cannot be seen or foreseen to be useful in the economic sense of the term. But the University also has a duty to channel students towards disciplines where they will be able to find career outlets, a duty to select students so as to reduce the huge first-year crowds and to lessen the number of failures. Every university, socialist and capitalist alike, must work towards a balance between the degrees they award and the demands of society. This is not a matter of technocracy but of common sense.

As for the consumer society which is so much attacked by the *enragés* and the lofty minds, it is only because of the existence of this society that hundreds of thousands of students are able to get university places. The only critics of the consumer society who are consistent in their logic are those who lump the universities together with the consumer society as things they wish to destroy.

One last personal thought. Some of my friends who share most of the ideas I have set out here, have warned me of the ultimate consequences of my actions. They tell me 'You, who have for years attacked the conservatism of so many of your colleagues, will now find that you will be "retrieved" and "used" by the conservatives. You should have joined the ranks of the "revolutionaries" and guided them, rather than denouncing their deplorable but episodic excesses.'

I am afraid that this objection underestimates the gravity of the crisis. I am not unaware of the danger inherent in the present confusion. Some men who are essentially in agreement are for the moment in opposing camps, while others, who are basically divided, have come together for a brief period. But have I the right to ask whose fault this is? When the leaders of the U.N.E.F. and the S.N.E.-Sup. mobilize their forces with an eye on revolt and subversion, when revolutionaries try to impose a new dogmatism, when general assemblies pass absurd motions

186

on a show of hands, how can we fail to oppose demagogy and nihilism? Who is more likely to help towards the 'restoration' of the old order and to block reforms than those who accept structures which are non-starters and who will end up by convincing the administrators, the Ministry and the Government that the universities are incapable of using their liberty and unworthy of receiving it.

19.6.68.

The Liberal University in Peril

The community of the University has survived all the events of the twentieth century: the Popular Front, the defeat of 1940, occupation, liberation, the Algerian War. But it did not survive the May revolution.

Never, in 1936, 1940 or 1945, did that part of the teaching staff whose views coincided with those of the party or movement in power attempt to use threats or intimidation to force the passive, hostile or indifferent majority to accept *ad hoc* reforms or moral abdication. In 1940 the Vichy Government took certain steps which affronted some professors and bruised the consience of almost everyone. But even though the Vichy Minister of National Education was a university teacher, he was acting as a politician and not as an academic.

There were probably other injustices in the opposite direction in 1944, but there again the great differences in individual reaction did not seriously dilute the spirit of community within the University. In all respects that mattered, the teachers preserved a distinction between learning and politics. There was complete freedom of opinion and expression outside the lecture hall, and a sincere striving for objective or rational thought in teaching (even if this endeavour was not always entirely successful). Relations between colleagues were as far as possible kept apart from the passions of the political forum, and bound by an unwritten law which prescribed freedom of commitment outside, and political neutrality within the university.

187

Of course this moral code of the university community was an ideal, in much the same way as the Declaration of Human Rights is an ideal. The university code did not have supreme power over what actually happened from day to day. In some circumstances, for instance in the election of a colleague, the electors—the Assembly—were aware of a candidate's ideological leanings, and they took them into account, although they would never have admitted it. More often than not, especially within small departments, the voting was decided by arguments as to the professional competence of the candidates. (Whether the results were far-seeing or blind I do not know, but there again this is not the problem which concerns us now.)

No matter how imperfectly observed it may have been, the moral code was not without effect. Usually I did not know the political views of my *assistants*, of research workers with whom I was closely associated, or of students writing theses under my directions. There were some disciplines in which teaching could not be blind to party quarrels. A man who believes in Marxism-Leninism presents the doctrines of Marx in a different way from a man who rejects them; but most of them, as far as they were able, drew a distinction between *teaching* and *indoctrination*.

The teaching of sociology cannot avoid a certain degree of partiality by what it says and does not say, and by the manner in which it says it. But no one acting in good faith could fail to see the difference between the two sorts of practice—on the one hand the presentation of facts and doctrines without dogma and without excluding anything, and on the other the imposition of one doctrine, say Marxism, and the rejection of all other doctrines as bourgeois or reactionary—or, alternatively, outlawing Marx and Marxism.

In French universities until May 1968, the teaching was of the former type. Even in the socialist countries of Eastern Europe there are signs here and there of a return to the norms of the liberal University.

Some of the May revolutionaries, initially the students, and later some of the teachers, embarked on the course which leads to teaching of the second type.

Here again I implore my colleagues to stop and think. It is of no concern to me if the generation of 60-year-olds to which I belong is fairly soon eliminated by the 40 to 50-year-old generation. Perhaps it is right that man's greater life span and the impatience of the young should result in a swifter turnover of élites. What I *am* concerned about, and what the students, *assistants* and *maîtres-assistants* who have written to me are concerned about, is the protection of the moral and intellectual values which the University, despite all its faults, has been able to safeguard.

If the liberal University has suffered the *coup de grâce*, it was not at the hands of the students in revolt, but at those of that minority of teachers and research workers who took part in the movements which the students had started. It is due to the methods which these people used to 'intimidate' those who refused to overthrow everything, who refused to proceed to reforms while minds were unbalanced and while the activists were resorting to overt or concealed violence. For the first time teachers saw themselves both as academics and professionals of revolution both inside and outside the University. Outside, the leaders of the S.N.E.Sup. concealed neither that they were university unionists, nor that their aim was subversion (from 27th May onwards). It was quite without precedent that for several days they refused to recognize the legal government as a valid negotiating body. They were civil servants of a bourgeois state, as concerned about their salaries as they have been in the past, and yet they tried to overthrow the Government which allowed them all the liberties of which their colleagues in the East are deprived, liberties which they airily planned to remove from their French colleagues if victory should be theirs. And these people put out appeals for university solidarity!

The revolutionary (or pseudo-revolutionary) action of a trade union was a violation of the unwritten law of the community. But the methods used within the University itself were an even graver violation. It is of course true that many students and teachers wanted and still want to 'reform the structures', to use the current jargon. But really, who can believe that so many professors had for many years nurtured no other ambition than that of handing over to the 'equal-representation committees' a power whose nature, limits and ultimate authority have still to be defined? Who can believe that a vote by a show of hands in plenary or general assemblies is an expression of the free will of teachers and students?

Those who did not want to join in the game found themselves the target of fashionable abuse—'reactionary', 'mandarin', 'cop' —and threats—'in tomorrow's university there will be no room for reactionaries'. In a situation like this, the call for solidarity within the University serves as a means of intoxication against some, and as a justification for the moral resignation of others.

Dialogue and *contestation*—fashionable words. But when we come down to it, when have professors ever refused a dialogue with anyone? How could the professors of the old University have imposed a philosophy of the world and society when, particularly in the humanities, so many of them had more or less Marxist viewpoints?

The 'critical university', the 'summer university', the 'university of contestation', have nothing in common with the aims which men of goodwill agree to be desirable—to open the university 'ghetto' to the world outside (indeed the Equal Representation Committees and the Assemblies of teachers and students are running the risk of adding to the faults so much in evidence in the professorial Assemblies), to remind everyone that the University has other ends to pursue than its own self-interest, and to transform the often anonymous and hierarchical human relations within the teaching body or between teachers and students. But the advocates of 'permanent opposition' make no secret of the fact that its aim is to be an academic and political machine of destruction—by no means a new method of education.

We are back in a period which is in some ways like the '30's. At that time there was a threat from right-wing extremism, but the intended victims refused to pay serious heed to declared plans which seemed to be incredible. The doctrinaires of the 'critical university' are not yet a threat to society at large, but they do not conceal their intention of destroying the liberal university. There again the intended victims are faced with plans so alien to their worlds that they simply refuse to take them seriously.

There is no question of rejecting the students' demands *en bloc* or of restoring the conditions which prevailed in the University prior to May 1968. (No-one would be able to do so.) But the advocates of the 'critical university' must be met with unyielding resistance in order to bring the majority of teachers and students, including those who were caught up, seduced or deceived by the illusions and the violence of May, back onto the side of reform and reason.

28.6.68.

The Wisdom of Machiavelli

The historians of the 'May revolution' have two choices of interpretation. They can ascribe to Gaullism either the responsibility for causing the events, or the credit for surmounting the crisis. The electors had to choose between majority and opposition. But this was a choice only in theory, for the simple reason that no one believed that the opposition of the left—the Communists, the Federation, and the P.S.U.—was coherent enough to form a legal and liberal government. It seems to me that as a result, many voters were obliged, despite their criticisms of the Gaullist administration, to express a confidence (which they do not all feel) in those who were in power before the storm and who will have to cope with its consequences.

In many respects the events of May 1968 remain a mystery. Only the future will show whether they were merely an accident on the road towards modernization, or whether it is a matter of deep-lying forces which suddenly came out into the light, and which, after having plunged back into the shadows, will burst out again with renewed violence. But while we await the verdict of the future, let us stay in the realm of politics and not that of history—to adopt a distinction dear to André Malraux.

During the first week of the disturbances, the Communist Party condemned the Nanterre students; then it announced a twenty-four-hour strike for Monday 13th May, officially to protest against police brutality, but probably with the intention of regaining control over the ranks of the workers. A few days later there were the first occupations of provincial factories, and then, the C.G.T., which it seems, had not intended to mount a major wage claim campaign in the spring, unleashed a quasi-general strike of unlimited duration at the very moment when the Student Commune was engaged in its mammoth teach-in and the writers were taking the Hotel Massa by storm. Finally, from Monday 27th May, the Communist leaders launched their 'popular government' slogan, and allowed themselves to be drawn into making the general strike political, a move which they had for long resisted.

This recital of known facts leaves one thing unresolved. Were the Grenelle agreements which were signed by M. Seguy on behalf of the C.G.T., rejected spontaneously by the Billancourt workers, or was this rejection due to the young and to the activist movements, or to certain members of the Politbureau of the Communist Party who were opposed to the C.G.T. line?

In the absence of any interpretation—and the average voter has no way of penetrating the arcane mysteries of Government and Opposition—it remains clear that the Communist Party made a grave error, not of its own decision but under pressure of circumstances. This error was that it resorted to quasi-insurrectional methods without genuinely wanting an insurrection, which would have entailed the inevitable risk of intervention by the army and then civil war. No-one really believed any more in the concept of a general strike, a Sorelian myth which flourished at the beginning of the century. The Communist Party gave the average Frenchman the impression that it was seeking to paralyse the life of the nation, although it did not go the whole hog because it refrained from bringing the electrical workers out. Furthermore, as in times of trouble the alliance between the Federation and the Communist Party is like that of the earthenware pot and the iron pot, the opposition despite itself began to look like a revolutionary movement.

One need only re-read Machiavelli to realize the electoral discomfiture of the left. The error which must be avoided, wrote the Florentine, is to inspire fear and not to strike. The left began by inspiring fear, and then by one single action, in the space of half an hour, after a speech lasting a few minutes, it swore by all its gods that it had never meant any real harm (which, incidentally, is true). It was all a misunderstanding, the left announced. All we wanted to do was to put the students in the place of the professors, and to cause inflation by wage increases.

What possible reaction could the voters have to such an extraordinary performance? They could either be converted to Communism, or they could swing over to give still further support to the party of order, which for the moment is the same thing as the Gaullist Party. In such a situation, with the single-vote ballot in two rounds of voting, intermediate parties have hardly any chance, and shades of opinion tend to disappear.

Such are the consequences, which could have been foreseen several weeks earlier, of the revolutionary exploits of which the P.S.U. intellectuals are so proud. Gaullism has been reinforced at the polls; the Communist Party has been temporarily thrust back into the ghetto from which it has been trying to escape, and from which the interests of France demanded that it should gradually emerge; there is virtually a complete split in the unity of the left, and a moderate left government seems less and less likely as an alternative to Gaullism; the French economy has been dealt a lasting blow on the eve of the completion of the Common Market, and much of France's regained credit abroad has been lost. A fine balance sheet.

Some of the opposition may reply that the Gaullists will not be able to govern. The young people both in the Univesity and outside will resume their action in the near future. The unions will launch further strikes and industrial unrest while the workers will find out for themselves the emptiness of most of the alleged advantages they have won. All this may happen, although the worst is not always certain, but these Cassandras who may be clairvoyant should take care lest they be identified with the authors of disorder. The political party which created the Lycée Action Committees, which brings schoolboys of 15 or 16 out into the streets, is certainly not going to be content to wait for the 'desired storms' to gather of themselves. I persist in my refusal to believe that the reform of industry and the universities has anything to do with dragging the under-18's into politics or with the anarchist style of the Student Commune.

Let us make a propitiatory sacrifice to fashion and to hope, by considering the current formula of 'turning revolutions to good use'. The confused feelings which inspired the May revolutionaries wavered between a Poujadist nostalgia for a pre-industrial society, and a futuristic aspiration towards a post-industrial society which would be rich enough to be less concerned with production and more with the use of leisure, with culture, and with food for the mind. Unfortunately France is still a poor country no matter how the national income is re-distributed, and the major concerns of most Frenchmen are their jobs and their standard of living. Now international competition and the Common Market impose severe disciplines; some of the May rebels rose up against scleroses of society which must be cured, others against hardships which a society in search of modernization cannot escape.

If the left is not brave enough to make this distinction, if it clings to its dreams, and if it follows the strongest traditions and tries to sanctify its temporary madness, it may indeed come about that the May explosion will be followed by other upheavals.

If this happens M. Pompidou will imitate M. Guy Mollet, and will call the French left, whether with pleasure or regret I do not know, the stupidest left in the world. This is not, however, a guarantee of the intelligence of the right, Gaullist or not.

NOTES

Preface to the English Language Edition

1. Tournoux—Raymond Tournoux, author of *Le Mois de Mai du Général*, Plon 1969.
2. Joxe—Louis Joxe, acting Premier during M. Pompidou's absence.
3. Peyrefitte—Alain Peyrefitte, Minister of Education.
4. Fouchet—Christian Fouchet, Minister of the Interior, formerly Minister of Education.
5. Grenelle agreements—May 25–27. M. Pompidou held talks with the trade unions and employers at the Ministry of Social Affairs, Rue de Grenelle. The concessions he offered in an attempt to end the strikes led to an agreement, which was subsequently turned down by the rank and file.
6. Hotel Matignon—residence of the Prime Minister.
7. C.F.D.T.—*Conféderation française de travail*—French Labour Confederation—the second most powerful trade union, and not allied to the Communist Party.
8. *groupuscule*—a tiny group. The word was used derogatorily by the authorities to describe the student political factions (Maoists, Trotskyites etc.).
9. U.N.E.F.—*Union nationale des étudiants de France*, left-wing students' union.
10. P.S.U.—*Parti socialiste unie*, extreme left of social democrats.
11. *grandes écoles*—see Chapter 2, note 1.
12. *baccalauréat*—see Chapter 2, note 1.

Introduction

1. University Crisis—articles by Aron, published in *Le Figaro* 11.6., 12.6., 13.6., 1968; see Appendix.
2. André Philip—Professor of comparative social politics in Faculty of Law, University of Paris.
3. Civic Action Committees—Counter-revolutionary groups, accused of having a paramilitary structure, which sprang up after de Gaulle's speech of May 30.

4. Capitant—Réné Capitant. Gaullist deputy to left of party who resigned on May 22 rather than vote against the Government on the opposition censure motion tabled against it.
5. C.G.T.—*Conféderation Générale de Travail* (most powerful union, communist dominated).
6. The Algerian Tragedy—*La Tragédie Algérienne*, Paris 1957.
7. *La Brèche*, by E. Morin, C. Lefort, J.-M. Coudray. (Le Monde sans Frontieres) Fayard.
8. March 22nd Movement—Movement which started in Nanterre (see Chapter 1, note 24) under Daniel Cohn-Bendit, a prime mover in the student revolt.
9. Censier—Overflow buildings for the Faculty of Letters in Paris opened in 1960. It was the first building to be occupied by the students.
10. *contestation*—the act of opposition, of challenge, of criticism, of dispute. The students were in *contestation* with the establishment.
11. Alain Duhamel—editor at Fayard (French publishers of this book), and writer on *Le Monde*.

1. Psychodrama or End of a Civilization

1. Jean-Jacques Servan-Schreiber—Publisher of *L'Express*.
2. Man of Versailles—*Les Versaillais*, men of Versailles, were the military repressors of the Commune of 1871, known as such because they camped at Versailles.
3. Tocqueville—Alexis de Tocqueville 1805–59, French social historian, observer of 1848 revolution.
4. Intelligence clubs—political clubs which flourished in the France of 1848.
5. *assistants, maîtres-assistants*—the two junior grades of university teacher (see Chapter 2, note 1).
6. S.N.E.-Sup.—*Syndicat National de l'Enseignement Supérieur*, University Teachers' Union (left-wing led).
7. U.N.E.F.—see Preface, note 9.
8. Sauvageot—Jacques Sauvageot, extremist vice-president of U.N.E.F.
9. *Opium of the Intellectuals*—English title of *L'Opium des Intellectuels*, Paris 1955; London (Secker & Warburg) 1957; New York (Doubleday) 1957.
10. Pflimlin and Faure—both former prime ministers (at that time called *présidents du conseil*). Pflimlin 1958, Faure 1952 and 1955.
11. Algeria and the Republic—*L'Algérie et la République*, Paris 1958.
12. *Archicube*—familiar nickname used to describe a former member of the Ecole Normale Supérieure.
13. P.S.U.—see Preface, note 10.
14. *groupuscules*—see Preface, note 8.
15. Pierre Viansson-Ponté—political editor of *Le Monde*.

16. *La Psychologie des Foules,* by Gustave Le Bon, 1841–1931, French sociologist; published 1895.

17. Vilfredo Pareto—Italian political economist and sociologist, 1848–1923.

18. Proudhonism—the following of Pierre Joseph Proudhon, 1809–65; French socialist who had suggested co-operatives in management.

19. Avenue Foch—fashionable street in the chic 16th arrondissement.

20. Lycée Action Committees—revolutionary groups which were formed in the *lycées* in the first phase of the disturbances to protest against the war in Vietnam.

21. Geismar—Alain Geismar—National secretary of S.N.E.-Sup. (see Chapter 1, note 6).

22. Grenelle agreements—see Preface, note 5.

23. Barjonet—André Barjonet. Head of Economics and Social Studies section of Communist-run C.G.T. He resigned and joined the P.S.U.

24. Nanterre—a new university complex on the outskirts of Paris. Its sociology department became a centre and spearhead of student protest.

25. Matignon agreements, 1936—talks between Government, employers and trade unions in 1936 which vastly improved workers' conditions.

26. Touraine—Alain Touraine, teacher of sociology at Nanterre. He took part in the movement and negotiated with the University authorities during the night of 10th–11th May.

27. Comte—Auguste Comte, 1798–1857, French positivist philosopher.

28. *Ubu-esque*—after *Ubu,* a character in a symbolic farce by Alfred Jarry, written in the 1890's, who showed what happens when a brute obtains power.

29. Hotel Massa—headquarters of Society of Men of Letters.

2. The Revolution within the Revolution

1. The first important examination of a French schoolchild's life is the *baccalauréat,* taken at the age of 18 or so, at the end of a lycée education. A pass in the *baccalauréat* guarantees admission to the University. The cream of the *bacheliers,* however, may be able to enter one of the *grandes écoles,* a varied collection of institutes of higher education, including the *École Normale Supérieure* (a very superior kind of teacher training college), the *École Nationale des Ponts et Chaussées,* the *École des Mines,* the *École Polytechnique,* and so on. The *grandes écoles* tend, perhaps rightly, to regard themselves as in every way superior to the universities.

The *grandes écoles* are for the few. The many go to the universities. There is no selection before entry, and consequently there is a massive drop-out at the end of the first year. Those who survive can go on to take their *licence* after two years, and their *maitrise* after four. These degrees correspond, very roughly, to a Bachelors' and a Master's degree in an American university. The first advanced degree is the *doctorat de troisème cycle,* the third-cycle doctorate, for which the candidate must hold a licence, and must defend a thesis on a clearly-defined subject. The State doctorate (*doctorat d'État*), is a much higher qualification, which must be held by all titular professors in French universities.

All these degrees are awarded on merit—there is no limit to the number of such degrees which may be awarded. But there also exists a system of competitive examinations, where the number of awards made is limited. This applies particularly to the much coveted *agrégation*, which is granted only to one in three or four candidates.

The *agrégation* is essentially a teaching qualification. An *agrégé* has two great advantages—one, he is virtually certain of a post in an area where he wants to teach, and two, his salary-scale throughout his career will be higher than that of his less well qualified colleagues (*licenciés* or the *certifiés*—holders of the *Certificat d'aptitude pédagogique à l'enseignement secondaire*, or C.A.P.E.S.—the certificate of competence to teach in a secondary school). This salary difference is not affected by the fact that all three categories may be doing the same work.

A similar situation is seen in the universities, where a junior university teacher (*assistant* or *maître-assistant*) who holds the *agrégation*, has a better prospect of promotion to the rank of professor.

If the hierarchy of the French educational system is rigid, so is its syllabus. The programmes for schools and universities are laid down by the Ministry of Education, and although the reform introduced by the then Minister, Christian Fouchet, and his Director of Higher Education, M. Aigrain, were intended to give the faculties more control over their individual syllabuses, this intention does not seem to have been fulfilled.

Things are not made any easier for the students by the acute shortage of teaching staff, which means that they can have little personal supervision, and that a great deal of instruction is given by means of the *cours magistral*, a lecture course supported by cyclostyled lecture notes.

2. *mandarins*—a term applied somewhat derogatorily to some authoritarian professors and directors of research departments who insist on laying down rigidly what research their juniors do, even where the 'mandarin' may be less able than those under him.

3. *statut de la fonction publique*—Civil Service statute which lays down the hierarchy of the French Civil Service, its duties, salary-scale, etc.; all university and school teachers come under it.

4. Durkheim—Emile Durkheim, French sociologist, 1858–1917.

5. 4th August—the night of 4th August 1789, when the French Constituent Assembly voted for the suppression of their own and others' feudal privileges.

6. C.N.R.S.—The Government-sponsored and financed National Centre for Scientific Research, which exists to develop and co-ordinate scientific research throughout France.

7. P.D.G.'s—President-Director-Generals, used here to indicate the wealthiest people in France, who could well afford to pay for their children's university education.

3. *The Death and Resurrection of Gaullism*

1. Massu—General Joseph Massu, Algerian War Commander, at this time Commander of French forces in Germany. Massu was prepared to bring the army in Germany back to France, if needed, to put down insurrection.
2. Versailles exploits—see Chapter 1, note 2.
3. C.R.S.—*Compagnie républicaine de securité*, riot police.
4. *contestation globale*—total opposition, the ultimate form of opposition or contestation; see Introduction, note 10.
5. C.A.L.—see Chapter 1, note 11.
6. J.C.R. and F.E.R.—see Preface, p. xii.
7. Sorelians—believers in the ideas of Georges Sorel (1847–1922) who saw violence as the only viable weapon in the class struggle.
8. *Force-Ouvrière*—third most powerful union, which split off from the C.G.T. when the latter came under Communist control.
9. C.G.T.—see Introduction, note 5.
10. C.F.D.T.—see Preface, note 7.
11. For the significance of this statement, see Preface; *R.A.*
12. M. Descamp—Boss of C.F.D.T.; see Preface, note 7.
13. M. Monnerville—President of the Senate at the time (May 1968).
14. M. Duverger—Professor of Constitutional Law and Political Science, Paris, and editorial writer on *Le Monde*.
15. 'The 75,000 who were shot'—a story circulated after the war claimed that 75,000 Communists had been shot by the Nazis during the occupation of France.

4. *Gaullists and Intellectuals*

1. Ricardo—David Ricardo, 1772–1823. English financier and economist, follower of Malthus, more concerned with the redistribution of wealth than the creation of it.
2. Bloch-Lainé—senior civil servant (*Inspecteur Général de Finance*), author of recent book advocating various forms of worker-participation, called *La Réforme de l'Entreprise*.
3. 'Alain'—philosopher and writer of the inter-war period, whose books and articles in the press were signed 'Alain'.
4. *Action Française*—extreme nationalist movement, named after a newspaper of this name, which was suppressed in 1944, having supported the Vichy régime.
5. Lévi-Strauss—Claude Lévi-Strauss, Professor of social anthropology at the Collège de France; a leading intellectual with a cult following.

6. Foucault—Michel Foucault, fashionable author of *Histoire de la Folie*.
7. Althusser—Professor at the *École Normale Supérieure*; Maoist thinker with considerable influence on the members of *Union des jeunesses Communistes-Marxistes-Leninistes*.
8. Lacan—Jacques Lacan, well-known Parisian psychoanalyst with fashionable following; published book under title of *Écrits*.

Appendix

1. *Steadfast and Changing*—shortly after the Fifth Republic began Raymond Aron wrote a book with this title.
2. *Chefs de travaux*—supervisors of practical work in laboratories, etc.
3. general assembly—as explained earlier, a general assembly includes students, while a plenary assembly is composed only of teachers, research workers and administrative staff; *R.A.*